Overcoming Organizational Defenses

Overcoming Organizational Defenses

Facilitating Organizational Learning

Chris Argyris
HARVARD UNIVERSITY

PRENTICE HALL, Upper Saddle River, New Jersey 07458

Library of Congress Cataloging-in-Publication Data

Argyris, Chris, 1923–
Overcoming organizational defenses : Facilitating organizational learning / Chris Argyris.
p. cm.
Includes bibliographical references
ISBN 0–205–12338–4
1. Organizational change. 2. Organizational behavior. I. Title.
HD58.8.A753 1990
658.4'063—dc20 89–18330
CIP

Series Editor: Jack Peters
Series Editorial Assistant: Carol Alper
Marketing Manager: Carolyn Harris
Production Administrator: Annette Joseph
Production Coordinator: Holly Crawford
Editorial-Production Service: Grace Sheldrick, Wordsworth Associates Editorial Services
Cover Administrator: Linda K. Dickinson
Manufacturing Buyer: Bill Alberti

Simon & Schuster / A Viacom Company
Upper Saddle River, New Jersey 07458

Printed in the United States of America

20 19 18 17 16 15 14

ISBN 0-205-12338-4

Prentice-Hall International (UK) Limited, *London*
Prentice-Hall of Australia Pty. Limited, *Sydney*
Prentice-Hall Canada Inc., *Toronto*
Prentice-Hall Hispanoamericana, S.A., *Mexico*
Prentice-Hall of India Private Limited, *New Delhi*
Prentice-Hall of Japan, Inc., *Tokyo*
Simon & Schuster Asia Pte. Ltd., *Singapore*
Editora Prentice-Hall do Brasil, Ltda., *Rio de Janeiro*

Dedicated to the many practitioners
who helped me to learn

Contents

3. Organizational Defensive Routines 25

4. Fancy Footwork and Malaise 45

5. Sound Advice: It Compounds the Problem 67

Preface

▸ Morale, satisfaction, and loyalty have been the guideposts for building and maintaining the human side of organizations. In *Overcoming Organizational Defenses,* I show that because of defenses that exist in most organizations (private or public), these guideposts can become self-defeating and can actually inhibit organizational performance. In a defensive organization it is possible to have high morale, satisfaction, and loyalty because the participants can, without fear, distance themselves from their responsibility to organizational excellence. For example, in a large business organization the employees created norms that approved bad-mouthing the system and then decried the amount of bad-mouthing going on. In another organization, managers reported that they were disempowered and were helpless about empowering themselves. When provided a genuine opportunity to begin empowering themselves, they took actions that deepened their disempowerment (chapter 8). In a large governmental bureaucracy, the reported high morale could be traced to a shallow or superficial sense of responsibility that was rewarded by the bureaucratic norms.

We are realizing that in order to achieve organizational excellence, learning, competence, and justice are a much more realistic foundation than are morale, satisfaction, and loyalty. The first foundation, learning, pinpoints how errors are detected and corrected, especially errors that are complex and potentially embarrassing and threatening. Competence means solving problems in such a way that they remain solved problems *and* increase the organization's capacity for future problem solving. Justice is based on a set of values and rules—in this case, about organizational health—that apply equally to all employees, no matter what their organizational position. I focus on these foundations in *Overcoming Organizational Defenses.*

This book takes direct aim at organizational defenses. It uncovers what is often known privately in organizations about defenses but is bypassed and covered up. I want to make the undiscussable discussable.

This book is for thoughtful managers and graduate students who want to reduce the pollution created by organizational defenses. It is also for consultants, in any field, who are dedicated to providing value added by helping clients to solve their problems. Management consulting, a profession that is growing at a fast rate, should focus on identifying and eradicating organizational defenses because they, more than any other factor, are likely to diminish the value the consultants can add for their clients. The book is intended for courses in organizational development, organizational behavior, and human resources. It is also intended to be used in courses that teach strategy, accounting, finance, manufacturing, marketing, and information technology.

The ideas in *Overcoming Organizational Defenses* have been developed over years of inquiry. Some were introduced decades ago; some with this book. The primary contribution of this book is to integrate the ideas into conceptual maps that can be used to generalize to many organizations and also can be used to understand a specific, individual case.

To date, the overwhelming focuses of the work on learning about organizational defenses are to increase understanding and to decrease ignorance. The purpose is to reduce human error that is caused by people saying "I did not know." I call this first-order error because it is the most obvious type of error that all of us, and our organizations, face. Parents, friends, schools, universities, religious establishments, and other institutions are responsible for reducing first-order error.

The focus of this book is on error that is less easily detected yet that, in my opinion, is crucial. I refer to error that human beings design. I call this designed error second-order error because it builds on first-order error.

Human beings are not usually motivated to produce what they do not wish or intend. Yet, in designing and producing error, they create this dilemma. Designed error is at the heart of ineffectiveness. Yet, we are developing institutions in such a way that designed error is necessary for their survival. We have a paradox. What discourages effectiveness leads to survival that is increasingly based on mediocre learning, mediocre competence, and mediocre justice.

Producing designed error violates the core of managerial stewardship. Therefore, producing such error is often covered up, and the cover-up is covered up. If human beings learn to cover up in order to help organizations survive and not to upset organizational players, they soon come to view such actions as necessary, practical, realistic, and even caring. Once this happens they tend to stop questioning the basis for designed error; indeed, as we shall see, they stop even thinking about it or looking for it. The practitioners become insensitive and blind and also become blind to their insensitivity and blindness.

Organizations managed with such mentality find it difficult to use the latest ideas of strategy, cost accounting, marketing, manufacturing, finance, information technology, and human resources because these ideas are based on rigorous and tough reasoning, not on defensive reasoning. More important, designed error and its cover-up are the foundations for producing unethical behaviors in ways that seem reasonable, if not necessary.

There are two ways to explain how these consequences are produced even though they violate the formal stewardship of management. One explanation is that the individuals are not aware of producing error while they are doing so. The other answer is that the individuals know they are producing an error but have figured out a way to make the error look as if it was not an error.

Skilled Incompetence

Both of these possibilities are likely. Individuals are not aware of producing errors because they do so spontaneously, in milliseconds. Their actions are skilled; they take them for granted. Moreover, as we shall see, individuals have theories of how to act effectively that help them to be blind when they are producing error. They have learned to act skillfully, and the result is incompetence (chapter 2).

Organizational Defenses

The second possibility is that errors are produced and covered up on purpose as nonerrors in conformity with organizational defenses intended to prevent players from experiencing embarrassment or threat. But such a reason has to be hidden. To admit that there is a need to cover up embarrassment or threat is itself embarrassing or threatening. In chapters 3 and 4, I describe organizational defensive routines in more detail and show how, for example, organizational defensive routines caused the communication problems that the Rogers's Commission said helped cause the *Challenger* disaster. The Rogers's Commission described NASA as an organization with a "can-do" attitude. I say this was not true about dealing with their defensive routines. I also say that the Rogers's Commission unwittingly strengthened the organizational routines that caused the problems in the first place (chapter 3).

In chapter 3, we also see how David Stockman and his group of bright and dedicated professionals were ordered to bypass and cover up issues that might have been embarrassing to the cabinet and especially to the president. We read how the Stockman team went from anger and disbelief that the cabinet was not the place to confront ideas to implementing strategies to bypass the problem and cover up the bypass, which became so internalized that they took the cover-up for granted.

Readers may be appalled that Stockman withheld his doubts about the trickle-down theory from the president for a long time. Indeed, there came a time when Stockman could no longer live with the cover-up, and he went public. Ironically, going public meant going outside the cabinet. This was a bypass that was not covered up. As we know, it was also seen by the president and at least by Edwin Meese as a sign of poor judgment and bad practice. The president took Stockman behind the woodshed. Apparently, the president never thought of asking what he and others had done that might have coerced Stockman to act as he did.

To complete the picture there are organizational defenses to protect the existing defensive defenses. These defenses permit a lot of fancy footwork to occur when the issues are serious and threatening, precisely the conditions under which an organization needs some clear thinking (chapter 4).

In chapter 5, I show how the best advice available does not deal with (indeed, it often reinforces) the causes of what is becoming a massive underground management activity. And the authors of the advice are unaware that they are reinforcing the underground management activity. Unfortunately, management consultants often collude in creating this massive protective blanket. They assert that they are helpless to do anything about it because engaging organizational defensive routines could lead to the loss of a client (chapter 5).

The time has arrived, I believe, to engage the organizational defensive routines, the fancy footwork, and the skilled incompetence. It is time that we stop bypassing and covering them up. It is time that we up the ante. The point I am suggesting is that we are winning the battle against error due to ignorance. We are losing the battle against designed ignorance, and that battle is the next one that has to be won. The most fundamental assumption of the underground managerial world is that truth is a good idea when it is not embarrassing or threatening—the very conditions under which truth is especially needed.

Fortunately, research and practice are leading to solutions that appear promising. I have organized this knowledge in a theoretical framework that predicts what is likely to happen and that can be used to reverse the counterproductive trends. In the second part of the book (chapter 6), I begin with a different theory of action to be taught to human beings. Once individuals have become skillful at this new competence, they will reduce the old organizational cultures, thus leading to the involvement and performance that we desire and also helping to make the progress persevere, if not expand (chapters 7 and 8).

There is a second positive contribution that I hope does not get overlooked. If the causes are bypassed, covered up, and undiscussable and if they are therefore difficult to manage, then it is unlikely that we will find examples in everyday practice of how these problems are overcome. Mapping the causes and how they become self-sealing is itself a positive contribution. It is the first step to making the unmanageable manageable. Time and time again, we have seen that the very act of producing a map of the bypasses, cover-ups, and undiscussables is seen by the players as a rare event; creating the rare event is itself a sign of genuine progress.

Thus, *Overcoming Organizational Defenses* as a whole represents a way of diagnosing your organization. Every chapter contains usable advice on how to diagnose the extent to which the problems described in that chapter exist in the organization. The book is more than a description of problems; it is also a guide to how to diagnose them in ways that corrective action can be taken.

I would like to thank Warren Bennis for his valuable comments.

Overcoming Organizational Defenses

Chapter One

Puzzles

▸ The message stated herein is full of puzzles, inconsistencies, dilemmas, and paradoxes. The reason for stating this message is that I want to alert the readers to stop taking for granted practices that are accepted as correct that, when examined carefully, are not. In other words, I want to interrupt the actions that are presently associated with skill. One way to do this is to show that embedded in the skillful actions are unrecognized puzzles, inconsistencies, dilemmas, and paradoxes.

I begin with three examples that illustrate how good results produce bad results and how the latter go unrecognized. The good results tell us that there is no problem. The bad results tell us the opposite. We practice management in ways that hide the latter and thus give us a false sense of security.

The illustrations come from three key activities of modern management:

1. Governing of boards of directors in private or their equivalent in public organizations.
2. Changing organizations in order to make them more competitive.
3. Increasing quality and decreasing costs in producing products or services.

I have selected these three activities not only because they are of major concern in most organizations but also because they illustrate several important puzzles. The four puzzles are that (1) the activities that produce success also produce failure; (2) how the success is framed covers up the failure; (3) the criteria of success in all three cases are not tough enough to deal with the problems that plague managers at all levels in many different kinds of organizations; and (4) in all cases, the players involved are not getting at the basic causes of the problems. They are solving problems in superficial ways, and they are unrealizingly kidding themselves that this is not so.

The ideas in good currency about how to evaluate management effectiveness are incomplete and misleading. They can be used to identify success and, unrealizingly, to cover up failure. Management, I try to show, creates organizations that learn how to correct the superficial problem in ways that cover up the superficiality of the organizational learning that is going on.

The puzzles therefore are not simply illustrations of interesting intellectual issues. They are signs of weakness of modern management technology and behavior used to solve problems that contain embarrassment or threat. The puzzles mean that buried deep in organizations is the capacity to be overprotective and antilearning *and* to be unaware that this is the case—*and* to do all this precisely when organizations need the opposite capacity. That is, when the problems are tough and are also embarrassing or threatening.

Board Governance and Dynamics

Lorsch and MacIver (1989) interviewed in depth 100 outside directors from the Standard & Poor's 400 companies. They also sent a questionnaire to 4,000 outside board members. The response rate was 32 percent.

Most participants reported that they had worked out a satisfactory relationship with the CEO and each other. Most said that they felt free during the board meeting to say whatever they wanted to say. Most reported that participating on boards provided opportunities to learn and also challenges. In short, board governance appeared in good health.

However, as the authors carefully dug into their data, they found some fascinating puzzles.

For example:

The Board Members Said:	*Lorsch and MacIver Documented:*
1. They feel free to say whatever they wish.	1. They are rarely openly critical during board meetings even when they are dissatisfied. They criticize indirectly and diplomatically.

The Board Members Said:	*Lorsch and MacIver Documented:*
2. They take their accountability very seriously. They have a satisfactory relationship with the CEO and with each other. They do not see themselves as patsies.	2. For the most part, members do not discuss their accountability among themselves. The CEOs control their boards by defining the agenda, and such control is rarely discussable during the meeting. The directors do not have sufficient power to carry out their defined responsibilities and they permit this condition to continue. In the actual cases reported, the directors were slow in confronting the issues; and when they did, they did so first outside the board meetings and later brought the discussions inside.

If Lorsch and MacIver are correct, why do the directors feel confident and competent that they are properly exercising their stewardship and yet create and maintain board relationships that lead them to have inadequate power? To dramatize a bit, why are effectiveness and inadequate power placed side by side? Why are these issues rarely discussed during board meetings?

One answer to these questions is that there may be aboveground and underground dynamics that go on during board meetings. The aboveground dynamics are used to deal with the routine issues. The underground dynamics are activated whenever the business results are hot and threatening. Everyone knows the underground dynamics; they are taken for granted. Also taken for granted are the facts that the underground dynamics (during the meeting) are undiscussable and that their undiscussability also is undiscussable.

But how do underground dynamics arise? In the literature on how to be a good board member, I could not find any advice on how to create, go along with and/or reinforce underground dynamics. More important, how do boards ever get into the position in which they create dynamics that by their views are both ineffective and taken for granted? These conditions violate the stewardship of board membership.

Organizational Change Programs

Over a period of three years, Beer, Eisenstat, and Spector (1988) studied six large corporations that invested heavily in change programs to help them become more competitive. The authors describe how each company had managed itself into an uncompetitive position. In looking carefully at what was going on, they found policies and practices that led to:

- Inflexible and unadaptive rules.
- Managers and workers out of touch with customer needs.
- Managers who were not committed, not cooperative, and often not competent to produce change.
- Poor interaction among functional groups.
- Top management refusing to believe that lower revenues and market share were more than a temporary perturbation.
- Lack of strategic thinking.
- Lower level employees not fully informed.
- Low levels of trust.

Why is it that well-educated and well-intentioned managers, at all levels, produced these policies and practices? Again, these practices violate the most basic features of managerial stewardship. Answers such as they were unaware or they drifted into these practices may be true, but they are not satisfactory. We need to learn what caused the unawareness and the drift.

Beer, Eisenstat, and Spector also reported that most of the programs intended to change the organizations either failed or had limited success. Indeed, even in the program judged to be the most successful, there was little sign of change at the top and some signs that after several years the change program may have reached its limits. Indeed, most of the programs began with a big fanfare and, like old soldiers, they faded away.

Why? Because, the authors state, most of the programs were packaged. Many were guided by off-the-shelf products that were not intimately connectable with what was really going on in the organization. Most of the programs were designed for quick success and the quick fix. The focus of these programs was on changing what the root causes produced rather than the root causes themselves.

Again, why were such programs selected in the first place? Because companies emulated the programs other companies used. These programs were easy to sell to line management because they were likely to produce immediate results that top management would applaud. What causes management to encourage such solutions?

Cost Reduction

Twelve foremen were trying to uncover where cost reductions might be made. In an hour or so, they were able to identify more than thirty areas.

Next, they ranked these areas for possible action. Finally, they selected six areas on which they promised to take action.

After three months, the foremen met to report their accomplishments. Objectives for all six areas had been achieved. Management estimated the likely savings to be about $210,000.00. Everyone was delighted. The mood was understandably festive. The group turned to champagne and dinner that top management had provided.

However, a crucial question had not been asked. Indeed, the manager who led the discussion said that he would not have even thought of asking the question. An outside observer studying these cost-reduction meetings asked:

> OBSERVER: Do you remember the list of areas that you identified three months ago?
>
> FOREMEN: Of course.
>
> OBSERVER: How long did you know about these lists?
>
> FOREMEN: We don't understand. What are you driving at?
>
> OBSERVER: How long did you know that these problem areas existed?
>
> FOREMEN: From one to three years. It was common knowledge.
>
> OBSERVER: What led you not to take action until these seminars? What prevented you from taking these actions without the stimulation from the seminar?
>
> FOREMEN: Are you kidding? Are you serious?
>
> OBSERVER: I am not kidding; I am serious. What prevented you from correcting problems that you knew about for years?
>
> FOREMEN: Be careful. You're opening up a can of worms! (*Turning to the top management representative*) Do you want us to answer that question? It could spoil the evening.

Reflecting on this story, we see that the criterion for success was a fix that was quick and easily measurable. The cost-reduction program was judged a success. However, the big question was not asked by those who managed it.

The change programs also focused on the quick fix and the cosmetic. They also used a cosmetic measuring process that produced hard numbers that, over time, became soft. The only thing that was hard was that most of the programs never met their objectives and faded out.

The board problems have, to date, never been dealt with. It is as if top management understands the depth of the problem and also understands the limits of most change programs. Top managers do not mind unleashing these programs on employees below them, but they do not want these programs unleashed on themselves, either within their organization or at the top of other organizations.

The players in these studies also take for granted policies and practices that are contrary to their managerial stewardship. They bypass root causes. They equate being realistic with being simplistic. They make all these actions undiscussable. They thus wind up creating a world in which the bad is tied up with the good so that producing the latter guarantees the former.

Finally, all of this is being done with the best of intentions. There is no evidence that the players intend to violate basic management rules or the fundamental values in managerial stewardship. Indeed, the managers who lament the puzzles also report that they see no way out.

This book is about a way out. It is about making the undiscussable discussable, about not taking for granted what is taken for granted, about getting the underground above ground so that the unmanageable can become manageable.

Seven Worldwide Errors

Over the years I have collected seven errors that top management considers crucial and that are backed up by research. They are errors in the sense that top management believes that they violate the principles of sound management. The seven errors are cited and discussed here.[1]

1. Actions intended to increase understanding and trust often produce misunderstanding and mistrust

Executives often leave a meeting with the belief that an agreement was arrived at and a set of actions will take place. Weeks later, they discover that the commitments are not met. Typical explanations are that there was a misunderstanding, or that unexpected troubles arose, or that people are still struggling (and adding to the state of the art). When they ask why they were not told sooner, an equally evasive set of answers is usually given.

The top executives themselves can also be the cause of the misunderstanding. For example, I have worked with CEOs who are committed to involving their immediate subordinates (or reports) in such difficult decisions as allocating financial resources. The subordinates usually applaud being brought into the picture as a group. The CEOs soon find out that the subordinates are not willing to ask tough questions of each other. A session that is intended to be participative turns into a session

1. For each error discussed, a reference is included in the References at the end of this chapter.

in which the CEO is asking the tough questions of a subordinate while the others look on.

The CEOs understandably feel disappointed. They often choose to ease out of the participation because they see it as taking up too much time and as using executive time inefficiently (e.g., those who are there observing while others are being questioned) and finally because, the CEOs infer, their subordinates have neither the stomach nor the trust to confront each other.

In most cases, these issues are not discussed. Instead, the meetings are dismantled, usually on the grounds that "everyone is busy," and they have asked for "shorter meetings." The subordinates doubt the truth of these explanations. They interpret the withdrawal of participation as a sign that the CEO found genuine participation too threatening. The subordinates rarely test the validity of these attributions.

2. Blaming others or the system for poor decisions

Whenever important errors are discovered, people tend to find fault with others (throw the dead cat into the other guy's yard) or with the system (follow the rules and procedures, go by the book). People often use deceptive, politically sophisticated actions, hesitate to tell the truth (or massage it), and insist that no one is really interested in rethinking policies. They believe that positioning is more important than genuine inquiry if it avoids complicated and unpleasant truths or embarrassing and threatening feelings. The Iran-Contra hearings provided many examples of this type of error (Etheridge 1985).

3. Organizational inertia: The tried and proven ways of doing things dominate organizational life

New and threatening ideas are blocked with advice that Hornstein (1986) calls "idea killers" (p. 82). These ideas include "the boss won't like it," "it's not policy," "I don't have the authority," "it's never been tried," "we've always done it that way," and "why change something that works?" (pp. 82–83).

Hornstein defines "the rule of repeated action." "In doubt, do what you did yesterday. If it isn't working, do it twice as hard, twice as fast and twice as carefully" (p. 12).

An additional stopper of potentially threatening inquiry is apparent motion. If there is a problem, then assure others that action is being taken and a report is on the way. I remember a CEO being told, "Don't worry, A and B have gone to London, and C is flying to Frankfurt." True, A, B, and C were in transit. But their instructions were to stay at their hotels until someone figured out what they should do.

4. Upward communications for difficult issues are often lacking

Upward from the employees flows information about attitudes, expectation, and production problems—only to disappear into the triangle (like the Bermuda Triangle!).

Managers in the triangle have neither the respect for the rank and file nor an understanding of how better knowledge can enhance quality, output, and efficiency.

Managers either think that their bosses do not want to hear employees' concerns or believe that is what the union or personnel office is for (Mills 1985, 52).

5. Budget games are necessary evils

Budget games include:

Foot in the door: Sell a new program modestly. Conceal its real magnitude.
Hidden ball: Conceal a politically unattractive program within an attractive one.
Divide and conquer: Seek approval of a budget request from more than one supervisor.
Distraction: Base a specific request on the premise that an overall program has been approved when this is not in fact the case.
It's free: Argue that someone else will pay for the project so the organization might as well approve it.
Razzle-dazzle: Support the request with voluminous data, but arranged in such a way that their significance is not clear.
Delayed buck: Submit the data late, arguing that the budget guidelines required so much detailed calculation that the job could not be done on time (Anthony and Young 1984, 377–382).
Our program is priceless: It is difficult to argue against defense or human life.
It can't be measured: The real benefit is subjective.
Tomorrow and tomorrow: If there are no results today, promise some in the future.
Stretching things: The real skill is not simply to promise something that is difficult to prove; promise something that is impossible to disprove.
Both ends against the middle: Play competing committees against each other (Wildasky 1964, 88–123).

6. People do not behave reasonably, even when it is in their best interest

People do not behave reasonably when they are faced with facts that are upsetting. Some of the most common defenses people use when in difficulty include these:

- There is nothing wrong with us that a long production run wouldn't cure (rejection).
- Tomorrow we'll get organized and plan (procrastination).
- Death in the drawer (indecision).
- Paralysis by analysis (lack of implementation follow-up).
- The more paint we sell, the more money we lose (strategic ineffectiveness).
- What the boss doesn't know won't hurt him (sabotage).
- Let's get back to real work (regression). (Ansoff 1984, 389)

7. The management team is often a myth

Many executives emphasize the importance of team work and team building. Thousands of hours and millions of dollars are spent on building them. The results, however, are in doubt. Peterfreund (1986) concluded that many leaders persistently make references to "our management team," yet there is no "management team"; it's a myth; more often, such references perpetuate a legend rather than create reality.

More Puzzles

The first puzzle is why do human beings produce, adhere to, and proliferate errors? Why are these errors described as inevitable, and yet there are, to my knowledge, no formal organizational policies that encourage or protect them? Nor are there executive educational programs within organizations or at universities that teach individuals to produce such errors, and to do so in such a way that they are predictably inevitable.

The second puzzle is that these errors eat up precious executive time and energy. Why do sensible human beings create worlds that have, by their own standards, nonsensible consequences? How did they ever get into the position of working hard to reduce errors yet have the main result be that the human beings get frustrated while the errors flourish? Indeed, as I hope to show, the errors feed on and strengthen themselves on human misery.

The third puzzle is that, theoretically, none of this should happen. Human beings do not knowingly design and produce errors. For example, research indicates that individuals design their actions and they design the implementation of these actions (Argyris and Schon 1974).

It follows that it is not possible for human beings to design and knowingly produce error. If I design an error or mismatch and produce it, that is a match. But the seven problems are errors, and they are worldwide. How can we explain this puzzle?

The bottom line to all the examples and the puzzles is this: Managements, at all levels, in many organizations, create, by their own choice, a world that is contrary to what they say they prefer and contrary to the managerial stewardship they espouse. It is as if they are compulsively tied to a set of processes that prevent them from changing what they believe they should change. If this is true, then management could be in a very fundamental sense not in control.

I believe these conjectures are true; management has created them, and the conjectures can be turned around.

Defensive Reasoning

Let's begin with how managers must be thinking and reasoning. Whenever individuals or organizations are free to act as they wish and yet choose to act in ways contrary to their own interests, there is defensive reasoning going on.

Defensive reasoning occurs when individuals (1) hold premises the validity of which is questionable yet they think it is not, (2) make inferences that do not necessarily follow from the premises yet they think they do, and (3) reach conclusions that they believe they have tested carefully yet they have not because the way they have been framed makes them untestable.

For example, the premises that budget politics are necessary evils or that the not-invented-here attitudes are inevitable lead to inferences that management must be resigned to these politics and attitudes and that little can be done to eradicate them. Holding these premises and believing the inferences are true lead to all sorts of actions that bypass and cover up the causes. Not surprisingly, the organizational change programs rarely address them or, if they do, the strategy is superficial and a quick fix.

But, human beings do not have to use defensive reasoning. The human mind does not require it. Why is it so prevalent, especially when dealing with issues and errors that are or can be embarrassing or threatening?

There are four causes of the defensive reasoning found in executives' action, especially when executives are dealing with business issues that are embarrassing or threatening. These causes are (1) the human programs the executives hold about dealing with embarrassment or threat, (2) the fact that they use those programs skillfully, (3) the organizational defense routines that result, and (4) the organizational fancy footwork used to protect the defensive routines. These four causes of defensive reasoning are the subjects of the next two chapters.

References

Ansoff, H. Igor. 1984. *Implanting Strategic Change.* Englewood Cliffs, N.J., Prentice-Hall International.

Anthony, Robert N., and David W. Young. 1984. *Management Control in Non-profit Organizations.* Homewood, Ill.: Richard D. Irwin.

Argyris, Chris, and Donald Schon. 1974. *Theory in Practice.* San Francisco: Jossey-Bass.

Beer, Michael, Russell Eisenstat, and Bert Spector. 1988. *The Critical Path to Change: Developing the Competitive Organization.* Boston: Harvard Business School Press.

Etheridge, Lloyd S. 1985. *Can Governments Learn?* New York: Pergamon Press.

Hornstein, Harvey. 1986. *Managerial Courage.* New York: John Wiley.

Lorsch, Jay W., and Elizabeth A. MacIver. 1989. *Pawns or Potentates: A Study of Corporate Governance.* Boston: Harvard Business School Press.

Mills, D. Quinn. 1985. *The New Competitors.* New York: John Wiley.

Peterfreund, Stanley. Sept. 1986. "Managing Change: Fight, Team, Fight," Stanley Peterfreund Assoc., Inc., 1–8.

Wildasky, Aaron. 1964. *The Politics of the Budgetary Process.* Boston: Little, Brown and Co.

Chapter Two

Human Theories of Control: Skilled Incompetence

▸ We can think of human beings as having been taught, early in life, how to act in ways to be in control, especially when they are dealing with issues that can be embarrassing or threatening. People transform these lessons into theories of action. The theories of action, in turn, contain rules that are used to design and implement the actions in everyday life.

The society in which human beings live supports the actions through social virtues, such as caring, support, honesty, and integrity. This chapter shows how the theories of action and the social virtues combine to encourage defensive reasoning and actions that are skillful and that simultaneously produce consequences that are not intended. Moreover, human beings are often unaware that they are producing such unintended consequences.

Model I Theory-in-Use

Human beings seek to be in command of their actions. They feel good when they are able to produce the consequences that they intend. They abhor feeling or being out of control.

Human begins have programs in their heads about how to be in control, especially when they face embarrassment or threat, two conditions that could lead them to get out of control. These programs exist in the human mind in two very different ways.

The first way is the set of beliefs and values people hold about how to manage their lives. The second way is the actual rules they use to manage their beliefs. We call the first, their espoused theories of action; the second, their theories-in-use.

It is possible to model the theories-in-use. Luckily, it turns out that the theories-in-use do not vary widely. Young or old, female or male, minority or majority, wealthy or poor, well-educated or poorly educated—all people use the same theory-in-use. The actual behaviors individuals produce to implement their theories differ widely, but the theory of design they hold does not (Argyris and Schon 1974; Argyris 1982, 1985).

Theories-in-use are the master programs that individuals hold in order to be in control. Model I theory-in-use instructs individuals to seek to be in unilateral control, to win, and not to upset people. It recommends action strategies that are primarily selling and persuading and, when necessary, strategies that save their own and others' face.

Carrying out these action strategies effectively leads to a dilemma and a paradox. The dilemma is that it is not possible to save someone's face and tell the person that is your intention. If you say, "I am going to save your face," then you are not saving the person's face. Face-saving requires designed lying, called white lies, as well as a cover-up of the white lies.

The paradox is related to unilateral, authoritarian features of the theory-in-use. In order for a Model I to be implemented effectively, the recipients must be willing to accept being submissive, passive, and dependent. These characteristics are the opposite of Model I. If Model I is defined as the effective theory of action, the paradox is that implementing this theory requires other people to act in ways that are ineffective by the very terms of Model I. It is as if the users say:

> I will use Model I to influence you.
>
> If I succeed, then I will control you and win you over. This will lead you to be submissive to and dependent on me.
>
> It is effective for me to make you ineffective. The paradox: If you were to act toward me in the way I act toward you, then I could not act in the way I intend. My theory of effectiveness will ultimately make me and other people ineffective.

How Defensive Reasoning and Actions Get Played Out in Real Life

I would like to tell a story that exemplifies how defensive reasoning affects the organization. The story describes the difficulties that young, fast-growing firms in the service sector often have in developing a sound strategy for the future. Most of these firms have been started by an entrepreneur who brought together a bright, dedicated, hardworking group of colleagues to market a new service or product. All of these firms have grown at fast rates, and some continue to do so, ranging from 30 percent to 60 percent growth per year.

Not surprisingly, these entrepreneurs all reach a stage at which they must try to manage their firm's growth and their organization more rationally, or many of them will burn out and their company could get into deep administrative trouble.

The CEO of one such company said recently:

> Right now, we offer products that clients can use that are prepackaged, off-the-shelf. The people serving those products are primarily sales oriented. We also offer custom-designed professional services. The people producing these services are oriented toward professional help.
>
> The product side is more profitable than the custom side. Yet the custom side is more challenging and helps us to design and produce new and better products.

I met with the CEO and his immediate reports, who supported his view that they must develop a vision and make some strategic decisions. They also told me that they had already held several long meetings. Unfortunately, the meetings ended up in disagreement and no choice. "We end up drawing up lists of issues but not deciding," said one vice-president. Another added, "And it gets pretty discouraging when this happens every time we meet." A third warned, "If you think we are discouraged, how do you think the people below us feel who watch us repeatedly fail?"

This is a group of executives who are at the top, who respect each other, who are highly committed, and who agree that developing a viable vision and strategy is long overdue. Yet whenever they meet, they repeatedly fail to create the vision and the strategy they desire.

If we go back to the criterion of incompetence described at the outset, the actions of these executives are incompetent in the sense that they produce what they do not intend, and they do so repeatedly, even though no one is forcing them to do so.

The Executives' Explanation of Their Difficulties

At first, the executives believed that the reason they could not formulate and implement a viable strategic plan was that they lacked sound financial data. They hired a senior financial executive who, everyone agreed, had done a superb job.

The financial vice-president reported, "Our problem is not the lack of financial data. I can flood them with data. We lack a vision of what kind of company we want to be and a strategy. Once we produce those, I can supply the necessary data." The other executives reluctantly agreed.

After several more meetings that resulted in failure, a second explanation emerged. It had to do with the personalities of the individuals and how they work with each other when they meet.

As the CEO said:

> This is a group of lovable guys with very strong egos. They are competitive, bright, candid, and dedicated. When we meet, we seem to go in circles; we're great at telling the others how wrong they are or how to solve the problem, but we are not prepared to give in a bit and make the necessary compromises.

I question the usefulness and validity of this explanation. For example, should the top management develop weaker egos or become less competitive? Perhaps these are the qualities that helped to build the company in the competitive marketplace.

A Different Explanation: The Source of the Incompetent Consequences Is Skill

Let us begin by asking three questions: Is the behavior that is counterproductive also natural and routine? Does every participant seem to be acting genuinely? Do the participants get in trouble even though they are not trying to be manipulative and political in the negative sense of the word?

The answer to each of these questions, for the executive group, is yes. That means that their motives are clean and their actions represent their personal best. If this is the best that they can do, then their actions are skillful in that they are produced in milliseconds and are spontaneous, automatic, and unrehearsed. Yet their actions are counterproductive. But the executives act as they do partially in order not to upset each other. These very actions, however, inhibit working through the important intellectual issues embedded in developing the strategy. Therefore, the meetings end up with lists and no decision.

We have developed relatively easy yet valid ways to learn about how executives reason and act when they are meeting to deal with issues that are complex, embarrassing, or threatening. We have developed a case approach as well as ways of observing the executives in action. Here, I use the data obtained from the cases that the executives wrote for a two-day session held off site.

The purpose of these cases was twofold. First, the cases allowed us to develop a collage of the kinds of problems thought to be critical by the group. Not surprisingly, in this particular group, at least half of the group members wrote on issues related to product versus custom service. Second, the cases provided a kind of window into the prevailing rules and routines used by the executives.

The form of the case was as follows:

1. In one paragraph, describe a key organizational problem as you see it.
2. Assume you could talk to whomever you wish to begin to solve the problem. Describe in a paragraph or so the strategy you would use in this meeting.
3. Next, split your page into two columns. On the right-hand side write how you would begin the meeting, what you would actually say. Beneath this, then write your response to their response. Continue writing this scenario for about two double-spaced typewritten pages.
4. In the left-hand column write any idea or feeling that you would have that you would *not* communicate for whatever reason.

In short, the case includes:

- A statement of the problem.
- The intended strategy to begin to solve the problem.
- The actual conversation that would ensue as envisioned by the writer.
- The information that the writer would *not* communicate for whatever reason.

The executives reported that they became very involved in writing the cases. Some said that the actual writing of the case was an eye-opener. Moreover, once the cases were distributed to each member, the reactions were jocular. The men were enjoying them:

"That's just like ___."

"Great, ___ does this all the time . . . ."

"Oh, there's a familiar one . . . ."

"All salesmen and no listeners . . . ."

"Oh my God, this is us ___."

One reason for the lack of success in meetings may be that it is unlikely that individuals will make public, in a regular meeting, what is in their left-hand columns. Yet, as we shall see, what individuals choose to censor has an important impact, because the individuals not only cover up that they are censoring something but they also strive to cover up the cover-up. The irony is that the other participants sense this, but they also cover up that they sense it and then they cover up their cover-up.

Here is a collage from several cases. It was written by individuals who believed the company should place a greater emphasis on custom service.

Thoughts and Feelings Not Communicated	*Actual Conversation*
He's not going to like this topic, but we have to discuss it. I doubt that he will take a company perspective, but I should be positive.	I: Hi, Bill. I appreciate having the opportunity to talk with you about this problem of custom service versus product. I am sure that both of us want to resolve it in the best interests of the company.
	BILL: I'm always glad to talk about it, as you well know.
I better go slow. Let me ease in.	I: There are an increasing number of situations where our clients are asking for custom service and rejecting the off-the-shelf products. My fear is that your salespeople will play an increasingly peripheral role in the future.
	BILL: I don't understand. Tell me more.
Like hell you don't understand! I wish there was a way I could be more gentle.	I: Bill, I'm sure you are aware of the changes (and explains).
	BILL: No, I don't see it that way. It's my salespeople that are the key to the future.
There he goes, thinking as a salesman and not as a corporate officer.	I: Well, let's explore that a bit . . . .

The dialogue continues with each person stating his views candidly but not being influenced by what the other person says. To give you a taste of what transpired, here are some further left-hand column comments.

> "He's doing a great job supporting his people."
>
> "This guy is not really listening."
>
> "This is beginning to piss me off."
>
> "There he goes getting defensive. I better back off and wait for another day."

If I presented a collage of the cases written by individuals who support the product strategy, it would not differ significantly. These people also would be trying to persuade, sell, and cajole their fellow officers. Their left-hand columns would be similar.

Reflecting on the Cases

In analyzing their left-hand columns, the executives found that each side blamed the other side for the difficulties, and they used the same reasons. For example, each side said about the other side:

> "You do not *really* understand the issues."
>
> "If you insist on your position, you will harm the morale that I have built."
>
> "Don't hand me that line. You know what I am talking about."
>
> "Why don't you take off your blinders and wear a company hat."
>
> "It upsets me when I think of how they think."
>
> "I'm really trying hard, but I'm beginning to feel this is hopeless."

These results again illustrate the features of skilled incompetence. Crafting the cases with the intention of not upsetting other people while trying to change their minds requires skill. Yet, as we have seen, the skilled behavior the individuals used in the cases had the opposite effect. The other people in the case became upset and dug in their heels about changing their minds.

This illustrates how skillful actions can become counterproductive; but why are counterproductive actions repeated?

One explanation is that the executives were una
to which they caused the counterproductive conseque.
doing so. The last phrase is important because the ca
the executives are aware that their problem-solving actic
tive and that they act in ways that, at best, produce c ... ome
executives can also identify the counterproductive actions ..e other people cause. A few can identify their own contributions.

But none of the executives were aware of producing counterproductive actions as they were doing so. For example, after they discussed the cases, they could see that they contributed to the ineffectiveness of the group and publicly admitted it to each other. They also made a commitment to change their actions. Yet, for the next several hours they continued their old actions. I began to interrupt them. They were quick to see what they were doing. My interruptions slowed down their spontaneous actions, which was the first step to changing them.

The reason the unawareness was repeated (and would have continued to be repeated if someone had not interrupted to slow things down) is that it was caused by highly skilled actions that were automatic, spontaneous, and taken for granted. These actions were in the service of being caring and thoughtful. "You just don't *say* those things in front of people." This is how we learn manners.

Social Virtues

Human beings cannot learn Model I without a lot of support from the society in which they live. The support comes from the social virtues that are especially important in dealing with embarrassment or threat. These virtues are (1) caring, help, and support; (2) respect for others; (3) honesty; (4) strength; and (5) integrity. The rules embedded in these virtues are briefly described next.

Caring, Help, and Support

Give approval and praise to other people. Tell others what you believe will make them feel good about themselves. Reduce their feelings of hurt by telling them how much you care and, if possible, agree with them that the others acted improperly.

Respect for Others

Defer to other people and do not confront their reasoning or actions.

Honesty

Tell other people no lies or tell others all you think and feel.

Strength

Advocate your position in order to win. Hold your own position in the face of others' advocacy. Feeling vulnerable is a sign of weakness.

Integrity

Stick to your principles, values, and beliefs.

We can now return to the executives whom I described at the outset of this chapter. They knew that they differed strongly; they knew that every time they discussed the differences, they became defensive. Therefore, they tried hard to prevent the conversation from blowing up.

They began their conversations in a civilized manner. They said what they expected the others wanted to hear. Each one emphasized the areas of agreement. They acted positively. At the beginning, they were careful not to confront others' reasoning. They acted as if they deferred to the views of the others.

They would argue that they did not openly lie, but not for long because they would admit that they did not say everything they thought and felt. They censored themselves under the guise of respect, caring, help, and support.

But this type of conversation cannot continue forever. The executives had to make strategic decisions that involved choosing how to allocate scarce financial resources, what kinds of compensation schemes to create, and what career opportunities to create for their employees.

As time ran out during each meeting and people would say, in effect, "let's make a decision" or "let's reach a conclusion," they did. The decisions or conclusions were in the form of lists but did not contain difficult choices.

This type of conclusion leads individuals to feel stuck. On the one hand, motives appear clean, commitment is genuine, and concern for each other exists. On the other hand, the actions that make it possible to believe that all this is true also prevent making difficult choices.

Moreover, if the members sat in the sessions long enough, "things could blow up." The reason is what I call the caring–integrity blow-up cycle. Individuals begin by acting in ways that indicate support, help, caring, and respect. These actions help people feel that intentions are clean, but little progress is made on the substantive issues. People soon feel frustrated and bewildered. They then move toward strength and integrity. They now advocate their position in order to win, and they stick to the principles. They act strongly in order not to feel vulnerable. As a result, the effectiveness of the decision making is reduced. Moreover, their confidence in their group as a problem-solving unit is also reduced.

The rule that couples caring and integrity with a blowup is: Start with caring, support, and respect; if this does not work, use strength and integrity. Under those conditions, the individuals who have the most power or those who can outtalk or outshout the others will have the last word.

These consequences trickle down the organization. Employees below hear stories of shouting matches, bloody battles coupled with some people keeping their mouths shut lest they get caught up in the fray. The lower levels then use these stories to explain why there is no progress and why the lovable strong egos are not going to make progress. Some lower-level employees, usually the better ones, try to distance themselves enough so that they can get something done. They may even make secret treaties with the other side, but at the lower levels, in order to keep the organization productive. These actions are often covered up. Such actions also may lead to stories that magnify and distort the degree to which the battles at the top are bloody. The distortion and the magnification help reinforce in the minds of the employees below why they must distance themselves from their superiors in order to keep the organization going.

Skilled Unawareness and Incompetence

Most individuals learn Model I theory-in-use early in life. When implemented effectively to deal with issues that are upsetting, embarrassing, or threatening, the result is defensiveness on the part of the players. This defensiveness leads to misunderstandings, distortions, and self-fulfilling and self-sealing processes. These are errors in the sense that human beings do not intend or prefer them.

But the errors are not caused by lack of knowledge or by ignorance. These errors are caused by the skillful implementation of Model I. If incompetence is producing consequences that are counterproductive to our intentions, then the incompetence is skilled.

If the incompetence is due to skillful actions, then we have a clue about why human beings are often unaware when they are acting counterproductively. The incompetence is caused by the very fact that the behavior is skilled. Whenever we are skillful at something, we act automatically and spontaneously. We take our actions for granted. We do not pay much attention to our actions because we produce them in milliseconds. Thus, the price of acting skillfully is unawareness. We could lose our skill if we were required to pay attention to our actions.

Whenever errors are due to skilled unawareness and incompetence, we must keep in mind that the errors are designed although we may not be conscious of the design.

Although we are not aware when we are skillfully producing designed errors, other people are aware. They are able to see us getting in trouble because they are observing the actions of other people. If they were in the production mode, then their Model I skilled incompetence would be activated and they would become unaware. For example, a team of senior executives attended a special seminar at Harvard to design a long-range plan for changing the culture and practices of their organization. One of the most important challenges, according to the team members, was to build trust in their organization. The team members were clear that this meant a change in the culture of their organization. They developed an action plan that was approved by senior executives from other organizations whose members were attending the same program.

One of those executives challenged the team's thinking and intentions on a key point. The team leader responded, "You're wrong. We have no intention of ___. Indeed, we expect to do the opposite."

I intervened to examine his automatic, spontaneous response. Most of the attenders, including members on the team, agreed that trust would not be built by such a response. He could have responded in a way that encouraged a dialogue. For example, he could have asked his critic, "What have we said or done that leads you to believe that we have the intentions you just described?"

Here we have a team that has been designing a program to change the culture and build trust. The moment one of its members gets confronted on a key issue, his response is in line with the old culture that he is committed to changing, *and* he is unaware that he is having that impact.

I should like to emphasize that the unawareness and incompetence due to our skillful use of Model I are not rare. One way to make my point is to return to the seven worldwide errors described in Chapter 1. If you are like most of the executives who recognize these errors, then consider the following statements.

- The errors would not exist and persist if someone was not producing them.
- Because human behavior is activated by our own theories-in-use, there must be programs of rules in our heads that tell us how to behave.

- If this is true, then we must have rules in our heads that tell us to:

  1. Produce consequences that you do not intend when dealing with difficult people problems.
  2. Hold other people or the system responsible for errors in problem solving and decision making, and do not examine your own responsibility.
  3. Repeat errors skillfully so they can continue to be repeated.
  4. Create organizational black holes in which information from below gets lost.
  5. Design controls of performance that make control more costly in financial and human terms. Conceal the rules and conceal the concealment.
  6. Hold assumptions about effective performance that make it less likely that the performance will be effective and that keep the players blind to this possiblity.
  7. Create legacies and myths that perpetuate undesirable consequences and that prevent individuals from realizing when they are doing so.

Whenever I flash this slide, executives express disbelief that they actually hold such rules. One way to deal with this puzzle is for them to say that the errors are wrong or that the theory of design makes no sense. Yet, up to the time they saw the slide, they agreed with both.

Another way to explain the puzzle is to attribute it to their skilled unawareness and incompetence, features that are true for most human beings.

Conclusion

Human beings hold two kinds of theories of action. The first is their espoused theory, which is composed of beliefs, values, and attitudes. The second is their theory-in-use, which is the one they actually use when they act. Model I theory-in-use is designed to produce defensive consequences and therefore requires defensive reasoning. Model I is also designed to keep individuals unaware of their counterproductive actions, thereby reinforcing Model I and the social virtues that we are taught early in life.

Organizations populated by human beings using Model I will necessarily be full of defenses that become routine because Model I is a defense-producing theory of action. Let us turn to examining the organizational defenses and see how they become part of the routines of the organization.

References

Argyris, Chris. 1982. *Reasoning, Learning and Action*. San Francisco: Jossey-Bass.
———. 1985. *Strategy, Change, and Defensive Routines*. Boston: Ballinger.
Argyris Chris, and Donald Schon. 1974. *Theory in Practice*. San Francisco: Jossey-Bass.

Chapter Three

Organizational Defensive Routines

▸ This chapter shows how Model I governing values (to be in unilateral control, to win and not lose, and to suppress negative feelings) and action strategies (to advocate, persuade, sell, and use face-saving devices) lead to organizational routines. For example, whenever human beings are faced with any issue that contains significant embarrassment or threat, they act in ways that bypass, as best they can, the embarrassment or threat. In order for the bypass to work, it must be covered up. The basic strategy involves bypass and cover-up.

Because most individuals use these actions, the actions become part of the fabric of everyday life. And because so many individuals use these actions frequently, the actions become organizational norms. The actions come to be viewed as rational, sensible, and realistic.

The results are organizational defensive routines. Organizational defensive routines are actions or policies that prevent individuals or segments of the organization from experiencing embarrassment or threat. Simultaneously, they prevent people from identifying and getting rid of the causes of the potential embarrassment or threat. Organizational defensive routines are antilearning, overprotective, and self-sealing.

A common organizational defensive routine is the mixed message. Peter Block (1987) describes several forms of mixed messages. Individuals say, "I don't mean to interrupt you," or "I don't want to upset you, but. . . ." These statements are designed to talk other people out of their natural response to our actions and, in effect, they tip off this intention.

Some mixed messages are organizational lies. Examples include "Thank you for the feedback," when we did not like it or agree with it; "I'm just here to be helpful," when we believe the others wish that we had not come; "We are glad to have you here," when we mean that there is no sound reason for their coming; "People are our most important asset," when we may mean it but have no intention of acting consistently with it; "I'm offering you a developmental opportunity," when we mean "We are not happy with what you're doing, and therefore we're moving you elsewhere" (Block 1987, 53–54).

People come to us with ideas and proposals, and our response is, "It's a very interesting idea." *Interesting* is the word we most commonly use to express either our indifference or objection, while acting as if we want to be supportive.

When we make proposals to people, and their response is, "We need to study it more," or "We need to refer it to a task force," or "We need to set up a committee," or "We need to check with other people to see how they feel about it," the other people may, in essence, be saying that our idea is not one that they can support, but they cannot tell us that they cannot support it.

Meetings are constantly being held to try to figure out how to communicate bad news in a way that people will find acceptable. The executives of a large bank decided to cut the corporate staff by 40 percent. Their feeling was if they told people their intentions, this would be demoralizing to the organization. Instead, they called the process the Delta Project and positioned it as a project to "engage people in the process of reexamining their function and their mission and their real purpose for existing." The individuals involved knew that the intent was to cut back on home office staff because the executives introduced the project by stating explicitly that their intent was not just to cut back on home office staff.

Kerr (1988) derived a list of "Ten Commandments of Executive Integrity." These commandments include (a) telling the truth, (b) obeying the law, (c) reducing ambiguity, (d) showing concern for other people, (e) providing freedom from corrupting influence, and (f) providing consistency between values and actions.

By the use of actual examples he showed how all of these commandments were violated in everyday life, how they were covered up and rationalized away in the name of concern for other people, for justice, and for just plain being rational. Moreover, he pointed out that all the examples were not unusual events; they were not carried out by competent leaders who were powerless to act; they were about decisions that were not made under great stress or pressures; and finally, they occurred in organizations that were not characterized as being in shrinking markets or collapsing industries.

All organizational defensive routines are based on a logic that is powerful and that has profound impact on individuals and organizations.

The logic is to:

1. Craft messages that contain inconsistencies.
2. Act as if the messages are not inconsistent.

When individuals communicate mixed messages, they usually do so spontaneously and with no indication that the message is mixed. Indeed, if they did appear to be hesitant because of the mixedness in the message, that could be seen as a weakness.

3. Make the ambiguity and inconsistency in the message undiscussable.

It is rare indeed for an executive to design and state a mixed message and then to ask, "Do you find my message inconsistent and ambiguous?" The message is made undiscussable by the very natural way it is carried out and by the absence of any inquiry about it.

4. Make the undiscussability of the undiscussable also undiscussable.

Individuals follow such rules all the time, and they do so without having to pay attention to them because they have become highly skillful at enacting such rules. The paradox is that this skillfulness is inextricably intertwined with incompetence because, as the next section discusses, the skillful use of mixed messages leads to a range of unintended and counterproductive consequences.

Inconsistencies and Dilemmas Created by Defensive Routines

To see the impact the defensive routines are having, let's consider the division heads who are being managed by mixed messages. The division managers must find ways to explain the existence of mixed messages to themselves and to their subordinates. These explanations often sound like this:

"Corporate never *really* meant decentralization."

"Corporate is willing to trust divisions when the going is smooth, but not when it's rough."

"Corporate is concerned more about Wall Street than about us."

The managers rarely test their hypotheses about corporate motives with top managers. If discussing mixed messages would be embarrassing, then publicly testing for the validity of these explanations would be even more so. The division heads are in a double bind. On the one hand, if they go along unquestioningly they may lose their autonomy, and their subordinates will see them as not having significant influence with corporate. On the other hand, if the division executives do not comply, headquarters will think they are recalcitrant, and if this behavior continues long enough, disloyal.

Top managers are in a similar predicament. They sense that division managers are both suspicious of their motives and covering up their own suspicions. If the top were to accuse the subordinates of being suspicious and of covering up their suspiciousness, these accusations could clearly upset the division heads. If the top managers do not say anything, they could be acting as if there is full agreement when there is not. Most often, the top covers up its bind in the name of maintaining good relationships.

Soon people in the divisions learn to live with their binds by generating further explanations. For example, they believe corporate encourages open discussions, but basically that corporate is not open to influence. They may eventually conclude that openness is actually a strategy top management has devised to cover up its resistance to influence.

Because this conclusion assumes that corporate is covering up, managers will not test it either. Since neither headquarters nor division executives discuss or resolve either the attributions or the frustrations, both may eventually begin to distance themselves from each other. A climate of mistrust arises that, once in place, makes it more likely that the issues become undiscussable.

Reactions to Organizational Defensive Routines

Whenever I describe these results, I get instant recognition by executives. They are able to give examples from their own organizations. Many ask, "Is there any organization that does not have these hang-ups?"

Once we get past the agreement that organizational defensive routines exist all over the place, we come to the question of why they exist.

One commonly held explanation is that they are caused by personalities or other psychological factors. For example, some people would assert:

> "You are dealing with fairly deep-seated emotional and personality problems. Aren't defensive routines caused by individuals who are incapable of interrelating with associates in any other way?"
>
> "Is not the problem fear of failure or an inferiority complex of who-knows-what but, in any case, a habit or attitude that isn't going to be changed easily?"

There are three reasons these explanations are unlikely to be valid. First, if, as executives state, organizational defensive routines exist all over and if they are caused by deep-seated emotional problems, then a lot of executives must have inferiority complexes and anxieties. I do not know of any evidence to conclude that most executives have these types of psychological problems.

Second, it is important to keep in mind that these defensive routines are rewarded by most organizational cultures, because the routines indicate a sense of caring and concern for people. The mixed messages around decentralization described above are created because individuals have learned early in life that these messages are thoughtful and mature strategies to provide support and caring on the one hand, and to minimize the risk of harming or upsetting people on the other.

The third reason is that we have been able to help executives to change organizational defensive routines without getting into such issues as anxieties and deep psychological defenses.

The Rules to Manage Threat Make Defensive Routines Unmanageable

It is not possible, to my knowledge, to deal effectively with any subject if it is not discussable and if its undiscussability is undiscussable. Under these rules individuals with a high sense of integrity and willingness to accept personal responsibility will feel that they are in a double bind.

> If they do not discuss the defensive routines, then these routines will continue to proliferate.

If they do discuss them, they (the individuals) may get in trouble.

One colorful senior executive told me that in their organization they called these double binds "s—— sandwiches."

The result is that defensive routines are protected and reinforced by the very people who prefer that they do not exist. But because the protection is covert and undiscussable, the defensive routines appear to the other people as self-protective and self-reinforcing.

Whenever actions are self-protective and self-reinforcing, they can easily become self-proliferating. The irony is that the self-proliferating features are especially activated when someone tries to engage instead of bypass the defensive routines. Once individuals realize that danger, they then shy away in the name of progress and constructive action.

Under these conditions, defensive routines flourish and spread into organizational loops that are known to all and manageable by none.

Indeed, the executives have told us that the thought that defensive loops could be managed is unrealistic, futile, or romantic. A few have wondered if such management would not be dangerous because, as one put it, "Wouldn't it mean that we would have to give up whatever we have to protect us?"

These reactions make sense in the world as it is. They are also self-fulfilling and self-sealing. They are self-fulfilling because they create the conditions under which it would be naïve or dangerous to engage them. They are self-sealing because they also create conditions under which to interrupt the self-fulfilling prophecy is not likely.

Hence, we have one of the most important causes of organizational rigidity and stickiness—defensive routines that get stronger and stronger while the individuals responsible believe it is unrealistic or even dangerous to do much about them.

Reactions to Defensive Routines and Loops

Because defensive routines are accepted as inevitable and natural, and because they are unmanageable and not able to be influenced, it is not too surprising that the most common reaction to them is a sense of helplessness about changing them. Employees in industrialized societies appear as fatalistic about them as peasants do about poverty.

The inevitability of defensive routines that is sanctioned by the culture also has a personal side. Individuals do not take responsibility for creating or maintaining defensive routines. They are willing to say that they are personally influenced by defensive routines but unable or unwilling to see how they may create or reinforce them.

One way to live with having little choice about defensive routines is to develop a cynical attitude about them. Cynicism leads to pessimism and doubt. For example:

"Nothing will change around here."

"They don't *really* mean it."

"I doubt if anyone will listen."

"Hang on. Don't get fooled. Next year there'll be a new fad."

Cynical attitudes make it more likely that individuals will ignore or sneer at evidence of positive intentions. Their stance is automatically to mistrust other people and to see the world as full of evidence that nothing will change.

It is a short step from cynicism to blaming others or the organization for any difficulties. And people will have plenty of evidence that someone else is to be blamed because they can see the defensive loops, they can see individuals acting consistently with them, they can see the cover-ups, and they can see that promotions often go to individuals who bypass the defensive routines.

Finally, people often give advice to others that reinforces the defensive routines. For example, "Be careful. You'll get yourself in trouble if you try to change . . . . That is a legacy from way back." So now we have the very individuals who feel helpless and cynical and who blame others taking initiative, becoming positive, and advising others to respect defensive routines and loops—the very phenomena that make it difficult for people to take initiative and to feel positive about organizational life.

The Stockman Saga and Defensive Routines

David Stockman joined President Ronald Reagan as director of the Bureau of Management and Budget because he felt that with Reagan, there was a decent probability that he could reduce big government and get the economy back on a free-market track. But the more he interacted with Reagan, the more concerned he became that Reagan did not truly understand how to bring about the economic revolution. Stockman and Reagan were committed to the same economic view, but Stockman realized that Reagan did not understand the important nuts and bolts required to make the changes. Stockman concluded that the same was true for most of the cabinet officers and the president's top assistants. Nevertheless, he thought that he should give an honest try to making changes.

Stockman's education and disillusionment began with the early meetings of the president and the cabinet. Often, the president did not understand the essence of the argument. Even more often, Edwin Meese (councilor to the president) would manage the meetings so that no thorough airing of views was possible, because actions like these were not discussable.

Stockman and his associates decided on several bypass strategies. For example, they learned to generate noncontroversial ideas for discussion during the meetings:

> We had to scramble all week to find enough of these "safe" items to fill Meese's Cabinet agenda while "big ticket" spending-cuts and economic forecast items receded further and further. (Stockman 1986, 102)

Stockman concluded that the tough decisions were not going to be made in the cabinet meetings "because Ed Meese was protecting the President from having to choose sides among his Cabinet members" (p. 109).

Bypasses like these have to be covered up. Stockman could not go to the president or the cabinet and describe his strategy. Thus, problem solving in the cabinet was reduced to mediocrity. Imagine also the impact on Stockman's group. They must have known the difference between big and small ticket items. They must have wondered why their bosses took up routine and mundane items with the cabinet. If they asked and were told the truth, they would have learned what is called politics. Translated into our terms, politics means designed mediocrity in order to bypass embarrassment and threat. The moment they accept this as facing reality they too have to collude and thereby reinforce the organizational defensive pattern. This education is real and powerful; it spreads like wildfire; and it is the basis for cynicism and a sense of helplessness.

Not surprisingly, Stockman had to devise a bypass strategy that would work over time and would not be viewed as a bypass strategy of Meese's and others' protection of the president's and the cabinet members' intellectual and interpersonal limits. Stockman hit on a structural solution often used by many individuals in his predicament.

Stockman proposed to Meese that he create another committee called the Budget Working Group. This committee would review all budget cuts with affected cabinet members before the cuts went to the president and the full cabinet. Even though Meese and Chief of Staff James Baker would be members, Stockman knew that neither of them would attend any of the meetings unless the president did. Meese agreed, and Stockman selected his team. It was this group that made most of the difficult choices.

The Budget Working Group meetings also became the setting for Stockman and his associate Martin Anderson (a policy analyst) to educate the new cabinet members and their staffs about the rigors of budget cutting. These meetings worked, according to Stockman, because the committee had on it several first-class free-market economists; and whenever there was resistance, Anderson knew how to cut the resisters down to size without humiliating them.

Unfortunately, Stockman does not describe exactly how Anderson cut the resisters down to size without humiliating them. People can sense when they are being cut down to size and also that the cutting-down is being covered up. They take the cue and cover up their humiliation and anger. These feelings, however, accumulate, and soon the players find appropriate ways to retaliate.

Stockman suggests that this may have happened. He notes that the cabinet members and their staffs began to resist. Stockman overheard various cabinet members talking with each other about his heavy-handedness. Moreover, cabinet members and their staffs learned to develop their own defensive routines. Secretary of Defense Casper Weinberger and Secretary of the Treasury Donald Regan were especially skillful.

Stockman concluded that their tactics were destructive of sound inquiry. Note what was happening. Stockman and his associates created a diplomatic way to cut people down to size. They also took safe agendas to the cabinet. These are excellent strategies to destroy inquiry into difficult issues and to create conditions for mediocre performance. Stockman concluded that it was the other people who destroyed sound inquiry and problem solving.

Imagine also what must have gone on in Weinberger's and Regan's offices. They had to retaliate in ways that blocked Stockman but did not appear to do so, or at least not for the purpose of cutting him down to size. They must have held meetings in which strategies were formulated and appropriate memos were created in order to win. Again, we have the people at the lower levels being educated about power politics and its undiscussability.

Trouble also developed because of the way the president was briefed about such items as budget cuts. The president reviewed the final results but rarely the reasoning behind the results. Although he could remember the cut, he could not recall why the cut was made. Whenever challenged, President Reagan would say that the cabinet was 100 percent in agreement, which in fact was not true. But Reagan never knew the browbeatings that the cabinet officers took in order to make the cuts. Stockman soon realized, "My Budget Working Group would prove to have succeeded only on paper, not in the real world of politics. The President never had the foggiest notion of why" (p. 113).

This is not an accurate conclusion. The Budget Working Group failed because the real work of politics (read organizational defensive pattern) that he hoped to create cut his group and him down to size. Moreover, and this is speculation, it could be that the president understood what was happening. Meese could have told the president that in Stockman, he had a diamond in the rough. Meese would deal with Stockman in such a way that he and his group would not become too disruptive.

Stockman also learned to make on-the-spot compromises in order to keep up the momentum for cuts. For example, after one meeting, there was still a gap of 44 billion dollars to balance the budget by 1984. During one conversation, in which Stockman and his group were getting ready to put out an urgent press release, Stockman decided that he would put a little plug in the budget called "future savings to be identified, 44 billion in cuts." This plug was dubbed the "magic asterisk." It too came back to haunt him, because no one paid serious attention to it. Everyone was acting as if the cuts had been made or would be easy to make (*Frontline* 1986, 7–8).

As the pressures increased, the fights and battles became more severe, and the players forgot how rosy their initial projections had been. They came to believe that their rosy scenarios were real. They had to, because "if we . . . had projected [publicly] large budget deficits, it would have been almost impossible to seek the program" (*Frontline* 1986, 7) with the Congress. Stockman added that he did not think that individuals consciously tried to deceive the Congress into passing tax cuts. "It was more a matter of self-deception. It is a matter of some idealogues, myself included, stretching credulity to its limits, being willing to believe something that was necessary in order to make a grander vision seem plausible" (*Frontline* 1986, 7).

This is an important insight into the impact of organizational defensive patterns. Their negative consequences on genuine inquiry build up slowly. Individuals learn to distance themselves from feeling responsible for creating defensive patterns. It is the other people who are at fault. Soon the bypassing and cover-ups become second nature. But they must still have to be designed and produced. That means that the players' reasoning process will work full time on these bypass activities. It also means that the efforts are highly skilled. If you combine blaming other people for the bypass with skilled bypassing actions that are taken for granted, it is not difficult to predict that Stockman and others soon would not only feel distanced from being responsible for the defensive activities, but also that he and others would become disconnected from their own reasoning. Soon the players are no longer paying attention to the distortions they are producing.

Stockman admitted that on reflection, he could see how it could appear that people acted irresponsibly, that they swept issues under the rug, that they made short-run policy and political gain based on weak facts (*Frontline* 1986, 14). But the actors, Stockman insisted, were not clearly aware of their own actions. "I don't think anybody lied . . . no deliberate deception . . . we were confused . . . but nobody said 'we know we're lying, but we're going to go ahead and do it anyway' " (p. 15). And later, "And we were all caught up in those daily tactical battles . . . we never had time to raise . . . the big picture doubts" (p. 16).

To compound the problem, the participants fight hundreds of administrative skirmishes and battles under enormous time pressures with escalating frustrations and disappointments. The impact of these frustrations and disappointments is additive, and soon the players reach a saturation point. They must now be careful lest they crack and lest their vision get destroyed. The emphasis now switches to short-term gains and short-term self-protection. There is little time and little appetite for self-reflection. To reflect on self-deception would only add to the burden. To take up precious time would be a recipe for becoming outmaneuvered by others.

Stockman held Donald Regan responsible for preventing the president from seeing the truth about the failure of the economic program. Stockman would lay out some figures, and Regan would warn the president not to accept them. Regan would remind the president that his program had not taken effect yet, that Stockman's worries were premature. Besides, if the problems were worse than had been predicted, it only proved what a devastating situation Reagan had inherited.

Stockman eventually gave up. "To be sure, there was no sensible basis for this assumption. But I wasn't even challenging it" (Stockman 1986, 286).

Soon, Stockman dreaded making public speeches, because he knew he had to pull his punches. "I couldn't really state flat out what I know to be the case, or it would have caused a new explosion in the White House . . . . Finally I said enough is enough" (*Frontline* 1986, 23). Stockman resigned and reflected:

> I didn't have enough wisdom in 1981 to realize that you could set in motion forces that would produce far different results than the blueprint required. And I think I'm as responsible for that as anybody. *I didn't will it. I didn't intend it.* [*emphasis added*] (*Frontline* 1986, 24)

I suggest that the wisdom Stockman lacked was not about the technical, economic, and budget issues. His friends and foes described him as a brilliant analyst and a hard worker. The wisdom that he and many of us lack is in understanding our own skilled incompetence, the defensive routines that we help to create or reinforce, and the sense of helplessness and hopelessness that we eventually feel as well as the predisposition to live with our self-deception in the name of trying to achieve some important objectives or visions.

Stockman explains the self-disillusionment as being due to overeagerness and too much self-confidence. I suggest a somewhat different explanation. The self-confidence felt by Stockman and most other brilliant analysts is in the technical area. Stockman may have felt confident in his ability to bypass the defensive routines within the White House, but the strategies he used were themselves defensive. He soon began to see what any bright and honest individual would see—that he was unintentionally beginning to deceive himself, to delude other people, to use defensive reasoning, and to focus on the noncontroversial and therefore unimportant issues. He realized that in order to achieve his objectives, he was creating a world similar to the one he was fighting.

It is this realization, I suggest, that is the most fundamental cause of burnout and of individuals' leaving at the upper levels of organizations. How can individuals live with feeling responsible for such inconsistencies? How can they live with the fact that in order to protect these inconsistencies, they would also have to lie, or at least to massage the truth about the vision and where the nation was headed? How can they live with the fact that they are creating administrative processes that are reliably unreliable?

What if the players could discuss the attributions they were making about each other that they never publicly tested, yet acted on as if they were valid? Stockman concluded that Donald Regan was destructive in the way he encouraged the president not to get discouraged too quickly with the trust as described by Stockman (*Frontline* 1986, 19). One could argue that the silence that Stockman and other like-minded officers used in order not to discuss Regan's impact, or their own, on the president and each other was equally or more destructive.

What would have happened if the cabinet could have discussed the rosiness of the original forecasts? They might have been able to go public in ways that would strengthen their cause. Equally important, such an exploration might have led them to question their own assumptions and to stop blaming President Jimmy Carter and other presidents for the deficits they were creating. According to Stockman, he knew by November 12, 1981, that the economic situation was even worse than he suggested in the *Atlantic* article:

> I knew we were on the precipice of triple-digit deficits, a national debt in the trillions, and destructive and profound dislocations, throughout the entire warp and woof of the American economy. (Stockman 1986, 13)

The American people are now and will for a long time in the future be paying for the skilled incompetence and organizational defensive routines of the Reagan tenure, as they have for previous presidents.

The *Challenger* Disaster and Defensive Routines

The *Challenger* disaster occurred in an organization that not only had a can-do orientation, but that also had in place voluminous rules and regulations designed to prevent such an occurrence. Indeed, the rules and regulations were so thick that ex-Secretary of State William Rogers was quoted as saying that NASA appeared to be "going by the book" to a fault. Ironically, the commission of which he was chairman added more rules and regulations and created an even thicker book.

In discussing this case, I focus primarily on the reasoning and actions of the Rogers's Commission and secondarily on the actions of NASA and other personnel that caused the disaster. I do so because the actions of NASA and of other people were consistent with the existing organizational defensive patterns. Focusing on these patterns would be repetitive. I focus primarily on the Rogers's Commission because I want to show that even a commission legally empowered to get at the causes of the disaster bypassed the organizational defensive patterns. I do not think that they did so because they were afraid or that someone told them to do so. I believe that the commission members, like most other human beings, took the organizational defensive patterns for granted.

I begin with the conclusions of the Rogers's Commission:

> Safety was unexplicably poorly dealt with given the attention, personnel, and commitment the participants had to the subject. A disastrous situation was developing. While NASA and the others were capable of recognizing and reporting it, the relevant players did not do so. The "can-do" attitude at all levels of the task at hand led everyone to focus on operational objectives. Once the focus was on getting the shuttle launched, the attention of the participants was diverted. (*Presidential Commission* 1986, 56)

The commission concluded that sound organizational structures, policies, and regulations were in place to prevent the disaster. Yet safety was poorly dealt with. People who were capable of recognizing and reporting safety problems did not do so. However, as I read the testimony, I see that the individuals did recognize and did report. The trouble was that the reporting was done in ways that would produce and reinforce defensiveness. The commission apparently chose not to focus on these actions explicitly.

Let us turn to the testimony for some illustrations.

Dr. Judson Lovingood (a deputy shuttle project manager at NASA) listened to the Thiokol engineers and decided that they were basically saying to delay the launching. Shuttle Project Manager Stanley Reinartz, who attended the same meeting, said he perceived it as the engineers' raising some questions, but they were not asking for a delay (*Presidential Commission* 1986, 87).

The commission members did not ask each witness to recall as best he could the things people said and the cues he got that led each to arrive at different conclusions from the same conversations. If they had obtained such testimony, the commission might have obtained insight into the reasoning processes the individuals used to arrive at their conclusions. Such insight could have helped the commission map out the ways that executives with different roles held different views without getting into hassles.

For example, the commission could have inquired why Lovingood and Reinartz did not explore their different views with each other, openly acknowledging how their roles might have influenced their perspectives. In other words, the players had the requisite information, yet it was not discussed. One reason could be the rule that exists in many organizations: Differences due to role assignments should be solved by taking them up the chain of command. Because neither individual apparently discussed his difference with the other person, which meant there was no reason to take their differences up the chain of command, both individuals knew they were covered if there were any difficulties, because they were thinking and acting in accordance with sound management practice.

A commission member asked Reinartz if he made the decision not to escalate to Level II. Reinartz replied yes. The commission did not ask him why he did not explore his reasoning with the group. For example, Reinartz might have said to the group, "I do not intend to take this matter up to Level II. How do others of you react? If there are any of you who feel strongly that I do so, I would be glad to carry your message to Level II or have you come with me, or you can go alone" (the latter practice is possible in organizations like IBM). The point is that in all cases, the information was available to reach a decision that would have prevented the disaster.

Roger Bolsjoly, who reported to Morton Thiokol, described his fears about the O-ring to his superiors and other people. They asked him if he could quantify his fears. He told them that he could not. He then testified, "The listeners on the telcom were not pleased with the conclusion and recommendation [that we were making]" (*Presidential Commission* 1986, 89).

The commission could have asked Bolsjoly what cues he sensed that led him to make this attribution. Did he make his attribution public with commission members in order to test its validity? Had he done so, and had the members confirmed his attribution, what would have happened if he had then asked his superiors at Thiokol, "What kind of data would you want me to present that, if I could, would change your minds? What leads you to believe I could get such data in time? If I am correct that you know I cannot get such data, then you must know you are making a request that I cannot fulfill. What is the purpose of such a request? (e.g., it is a cue for me; okay, but that bypasses the problem)."

If the data required were systematic quantitative data from studies that everyone knew did not exist nor could be done quickly, then such a line of inquiry would have helped make public to all concerned how closed the management participants were to being influenced. If this became public knowledge to their superiors, then it would have been more difficult to act in ways that protected the actors—for example, making contradictory inferences, as did Lovingood and Reinartz, and not making these inferences subject to inquiry. These actions are protective because keeping their conclusions private and acting as if they were not is a way for people to cover themselves. If individuals had lost their cover, they might have become more able to be influenced by the engineering data and/or they might have taken the controversy up the line. The top administrators testified that if they had heard the differences in views, they would not have agreed to launch.

The engineers could not understand why their recommendation was going to be reversed. They spoke out again and again to make their position clear: "When Arnie realized he wasn't getting through, he just stopped . . . . I also stopped when it was apparent that I couldn't get anybody to listen" (*Presidential Commission* 1986, 92).

What would have happened if the engineers had discussed the attributions they were making about their superiors' openness with their superiors? For example, after the management decision was made to launch, the engineers were asked if they had anything they wanted to say. The engineers remained silent. The management officials reported to the commission that they interpreted their subordinates' silence as agreement with the decision. What would have happened if the engineers had said, "We believe that we have been given the opportunity to express our views. We also believe, however, that our views are not being heard"? Such a comment might have led a management official to ask, "What cues were the engineers getting that led them to conclude that the management was closed?" This question could have made it possible for one of the engineers to say what he said privately to his fellow engineers *after* the meeting:

> This was a meeting where the determination was to launch, and it was up to us to prove beyond a shadow of a doubt that it was not safe to do so. This is in total reverse to what the position usually is in a pre-flight conversation or flight readiness review. It is usually exactly the opposite. (*Presidential Commission*, 1986, 93)

What if the engineer had said this during the meeting and then asked, "If you disagree with our conclusions, would you (management) tell us what is causing you to take this stance? It would help us to understand your situation better. It might also help us become better advocates of our position."

It is unlikely that any of this would occur given the fact that the engineers believed that to inquire into management's reasoning for taking the stance they took would be tantamount to questioning management's prerogatives.

The practice was to exclude engineers from management decisions. This practice is usually designed to prevent the escalating error, defensiveness, and polarization that might occur when individuals differ and deal with their differences defensively.

The engineers reported that this practice was *not* flawed. They felt that they had been given an opportunity to state their case. They emphasized in their testimony that they would not act in any way that appeared that they were questioning management's right to make the decision (*Presidential Commission* 1986, 93). Hence, giving up as they did and covering those feelings up were acts of reasonable integrity and loyalty to the organizations.

One Commission member asked the engineers if they were in the following dilemma: Even if they could provide stronger evidence not to launch the shuttle, it was unlikely that such evidence would carry because the previous launches did not fail. The engineers replied, "That is right" (*Presidential Commission* 1986, 93).

What would have happened if the engineers had articulated this dilemma to their superiors? How would the superiors have responded, knowing that the subordinates expressed the dilemma?

A member of the commission asked Senior Vice-President Jerry Mason if the comments by George Hardy (Marshall Space Center deputy director of Science and Engineering, who was appalled by the engineers' conclusion)) and Lawrence Mulloy (Marshall manager of Solid Rocket Booster Project, who said that he asked if the engineers wanted him to wait until April to launch) did not affect his reasoning. Mason replied that these comments might affect the lower-level engineers but not him, because he dealt with these kinds of problems all the time (*Presidential Commission* 1986, 94–95).

What would have happened if Mason had said to the engineers, "I believe that you do not have much experience with reactions by upper-level superiors (such as Hardy and Mulloy). I am interested in learning more about the impact that their comments had on you." This request might have helped the engineers say publicly what they thought privately, which was that the top managers were upset with them.

Moreover, such an inquiry might have helped legitimize the public expression of such feelings in the future. Superiors would then be on notice that the top of NASA would expect to learn about such feelings and how they were dealt with.

Two consequences of dialogues were that both sides stuck to principles and each side felt that the other side was closed and closed in such a way that it was covered. For example, the superiors remained calm, cool, and collected, and above the emotionality of the engineers. Because the emotionality was never discussed, the superiors could honestly testify that the meetings had been calm, cool, and collected, and that the engineers had had ample opportunity to make their case.

The engineers, having less power, had the choice to withdraw and distance themselves (as some did) or to speak their mind. Unfortunately, the one individual who spoke his mind was so frustrated that his remarks could have been interpreted by his calm, cool, and collected superiors as being too emotional and perhaps a bit unfair, and therefore as being privately discountable.

For example, Allan MacDonald of Morton Thiokol did become upset and told one superior that his view was "asinine." Later MacDonald said "if something goes wrong on this flight, I wouldn't want to have to be the person to stand up in front of a board of inquiry and say . . . I told them . . . to fly this thing outside what the motor was qualified to" (*Presidential Commission* 1986, 95).

Given the can-do attitude that permeated all levels of NASA, one can imagine that MacDonald's comment could lead the executives to put on their macho hats and take the risk.

We can now return to the commission's findings. The commission stated (pp. 104–105):

- A well-structured and managed system emphasizing safety would have flagged the rising doubts.
- The waiving of launch constraints appears to have been at the expense of flight safety.
- There was no system that made it imperative that launch constraints and waivers of launch constraints be considered by all levels of management.

- The commission is troubled . . . by the propensity at Marshall to contain potentially serious problems and to attempt to resolve them internally rather than communicate them forward.

These findings are only partially correct. For example, the problem was more than a well-structured system that would have flagged the rising doubts. The doubts were known but bypassed because people were following practice accepted in most organizations when dealing with defensive routines. Why would anyone have to make imperative to loyal, committed employees that launch constraints and waivers of launch constraints be considered by all levels of management? The engineers and other employees knew full well the differences of their implications. Why do they need rules to require them to communicate upward what they know are critical differences? Or, to put it another way, what organizational defensive patterns were operating when the managers made the judgment not to communicate upward?

Finally, the concern of the commission that potentially serious problems be communicated upward could become a recipe for people covering their asses (to use government vernacular). The same could be true for the idea that all launch constraints and waivers of launch constraints be sent upward to all levels.

In stating their findings this way, the commission makes it less likely that it will reduce the defensive routines and the defensive living system in place to deal with embarrassment and threat. For example, the commission could have come to the following conclusions: The participants believed that they had a well-structured and well-managed system emphasizing safety; they knew that launch constraints were being waived in the name of the can-do attitude; they knew they were violating the rules that make it imperative to communicative waivers of launch constraints to all levels; and they knew to take issues forward if they thought it was necessary.

The problems were not only in the structure, rules, and independent monitoring devices. The problems also were that highly committed, well-intentioned, safety-oriented, can-do players reasoned and acted in ways that violated their own standards and made certain that this violation was covered up and that the cover-up was covered up.

The commission recommended the establishment of a new oversight group that was independent of NASA, new job definitions for managers, astronauts in the decision process, a new shuttle safety panel, tougher reviews by an audit panel, and a new safety position headed by an individual reporting to the director (*Presidential Commission* 1986, 198–201).

These recommendations are understandable if the commission does *not* consider the skilled incompetence and the organizational defensive routines as being manageable. The irony is that its recommendations added more bureaucracy while protecting the existing skilled incompetence and the organizational defensive routines. The conclusions could have been made only by a group of individuals who, like all of us, take skilled incompetence and organizational defensive routines for granted.

Conclusion

Organizational defensive routines make it highly likely that individuals, groups, intergroups, and organizations will not detect and correct the errors that are embarrassing and threatening because the fundamental rules are to (1) bypass the errors and act as if that were not being done, (2) make the bypass undiscussable, and (3) make its undiscussability undiscussable.

These conditions, in turn, make it difficult to engage the organizational defense routines in order to interrupt them and reduce them. Indeed, the very attempt to engage them will lead to the defensive routines' being activated and strengthened. This, in turn, reinforces and proliferates the defensive routines.

Individuals feel helpless about changing organizational defensive routines for at least two reasons. One, they feel the change is hopeless because the cure appears to be one that will make the illness worse. Two, they do not wish to be seen as deliberately making the situation worse by opening up a can of worms.

The result is something equivalent to an underground economy—namely, a gray organization that is alive and flourishing yet officially considered dead or nonexistent. This, of course, makes it possible for the gray organization to remain alive and to flourish. We now have the underground management managing the aboveground.

Managing the underground management is usually known to most people in organizations through stories about defensive reasoning and action. One recent example was the story about the demise of Lehman Brothers (Auletta 1985a, b). The organizational defensive routines were so developed that the CEO, Peter G. Peterson, was shocked by the so-called betrayal of those he had helped. They, in turn, asserted that his shock was proof of this blindness. Many partners, no matter which side they supported, stood by in silence when one of their members, in a moment of desperation, questioned their moral commitment to the stewardship of the firm. The defensive routines and loops that led to the demise of the firm had existed for years. They were known by many of the partners.

The same is true for the top government officials involved in the Vietnam War decisions, even though they were The Best and the Brightest *(Halberstam 1972) and had produced important errors described in the* Pentagon Papers *(Sheehan et al. 1971).*

Several years ago, after a talk at West Point, I walked with the commandant. He wondered if I were not making a mountain out of a molehill. Individuals of honor and integrity, he pointed out, would not go underground in their relationships with their superiors. The officer was General William Westmoreland.

References

Auletta, Ken. "Power, Greed, and Glory on Wall Street: The Fall of Lehman Brothers." *New York Times Magazine*, 17 February 1985 (a).

———. "Power, Greed, and Glory on Wall Street: The Fall of Lehman Brothers." *New York Times Magazine*, 24 February 1985 (b).

Block, Peter. 1987. *The Empowered Manager: Positive Political Skills at Work.* San Francisco: Jossey-Bass.

Frontline. The Disillusionment of David Stockman. April 1986. Boston: WGBH transcript.

Halberstam, David. 1972. *The Best and the Brightest.* New York: Random House.

Janis, Irving L. 1982. *Victims of Groupthink.* Boston: Houghton-Mifflin.

Janis, Irving L., and L. Mann. 1977. *Decision Making.* New York: The Free Press.

Kerr, Steven. 1988. "Integrity in Effective Leadership," in Suresh Srivasta (ed.), *Executive Integrity.* San Francisco: Jossey-Bass, 122–139.

Presidential Commision: On the Space Shuttle Challenger Accident. June 5, 1986. Washington, D.C.: Government Printing Office.

Sheehan, Neil, et al. 1971. *Pentagon Papers.* Toronto: Bantam Books.

Stockman, David A. 1986. *The Triumph of Politics: How the Reagan Revolution Failed.* New York: Harper and Row.

Chapter Four

Fancy Footwork and Malaise

▸ In the previous chapter we saw how once defensive routines are created they cause human beings to act in ways that are counterproductive to the fomal goals or objectives of their organization. This chapter shows how the human beings come to think and act in ways that protect the defensive routines. People use fancy footwork that is highly saturated with defensive reasoning that not only protects the defenses but also adds an additional layer of organizational pathology, which I call malaise.

Organizational defensive routines create a double bind. If they are not confronted, they will reduce performance, commitment, and concern for the organization. Excellence will be, at best, an ongoing fad destined to progressive deterioration. If defensive routines are confronted in order to reduce them, there is a risk of opening up a can of worms because the players do not know how to do it effectively. Skilled incompetence, the logic of defensive routines, a sense of hopelessness, and cynicism are not sound bases for change.

Yet organizational defensive routines and their consequences violate managerial stewardship and accepted management principles. How do individuals live with the double bind? It depends. Individuals who are not committed to the organization, who have distanced themselves, and who have chosen to play it safe do not have a serious problem. They find comfort and protection in the defensive routines and their consequences. After all, everyone bypasses them and covers up the bypass. Who can punish these individuals for being realistic and practical?

The situation is very different for individuals who genuinely care for organizational performance, who feel proud to aspire toward excellence, who are committed, and who want to be involved. For them, the double bind raises all kinds of internal tensions because in accepting the situation as it is, they are violating their own sense of integrity. How do they live with this violation? Do they feel any shame or even guilt?

I believe that many people who are involved do feel frustrated and, at times, embarrassed. But they do not see a way out.

One way for individuals to deal with their pent up feelings is to redefine authority and responsibility (Baum 1987) in such a way that they can change the meaning of these terms whenever they are confronted with the possibility that they or others might become aware of their shame or guilt. For example, these individuals may espouse being responsible and taking authority. Yet, when a chance arises to reduce the organizational defensive routines, they redefine what authority and responsibility mean so that they can continue to bypass and cover up.

I call this fancy footwork. Fancy footwork includes actions that permit individuals to be blind to inconsistencies in their actions or to deny that these inconsistencies even exist, or, if they cannot do either, to place the blame on other people. Fancy footwork means to use all the defensive reasoning and actions at their command in order to continue the distancing and blindness without holding themselves responsible for doing so.

In order to observe fancy footwork we have to find instances in which individuals or groups have committed themselves to engaging the hot issues and situations and yet have trouble being effective. A key cause of their ineffectiveness is their own behavior, yet they are unaware that this is the case.

The following sections describe three examples of fancy footwork that typify many of those I have encountered frequently in organizations. First are senior executives who espouse that they want to build an effective and cohesive top management team. Second are professionals who decry organizational defensive routines and fancy footwork, yet whenever they try to reduce either they activate their own fancy footwork that reinforces the defensive routines they are trying to reduce. Third are the organizational development, management education, and career development specialists who, when under stress, act precisely in the ways that they, too, condemn.

Mr. Team

Mr. Team is always espousing the importance of teamwork and cooperation. He says, for example:

> "We are now too big, and the technology has become so complex, that it is unlikely that our company will make progress by depending on one person no matter how brilliant. Even if such a person existed, we now know that effective implementation in the future will require a team."
>
> *or,*
>
> "You are the single most important group in the company. You *really* control the family jewels. The future is up to us. The next innovations are going to be so complex and costly that singularly we are useless."

Mr. Team expresses disappointment and impatience with the progress made so far in building a team of his immediate subordinates. He has his doubts about whether *they* will become an effective team, but he covers up these doubts.

> "They have not become an effective team where they can discuss the difficult issues. There is hedging, and you can see that they hold back when it comes to the crunch."
>
> *or,*
>
> "I don't know why they are not effective as a team. Maybe they do not realize how important it is for them to become one. (*pause*) No . . . I really don't know why."
>
> "What worries me most is that I see a reluctance on their part to get together to spell out their differences and to work them out."

They bring the integrating decisions to him to make. When pressed to explain, Mr. Team reflects and says:

> "Maybe it's our culture. Most of my team has been here for at least fifteen years. Maybe they are victims of their culture."
>
> *or,*
>
> "When you come down to it, I guess it's people like me. When they come down to us for a solution, we give them one."

To use our metaphor, Mr. Team's left-hand column includes:

"I am trying hard. I keep pleading for a team."

"They are increasingly failing me."

"I must keep being optimistic and keep trying."

"It is getting tiring and disappointing."

Mr. Team deals with his increasing feelings of doubt and of being manipulated by censoring them and by acting as if he does not have these feelings. He reasons that he must "act positively" if any progress is to be made. He never tests this attribution nor does he communicate his disenchantment. All this is done in the name of being humane and not embarrassing the team.

When he is asked what cues does he get that the team members would be embarrassed, Mr. Team is either unable to provide any, or those he does provide could be easily caused by his own actions. If he is questioned further, Mr. Team finally admits that the basis for his actions is his belief that to discuss these ideas and feelings could harm and upset the subordinates. He is also quick to point out that he cannot test his belief because the test itself could make the situation worse.

There is truth to Mr. Team's fears. Some subordinates do become upset, because they, too, believe it could be dangerous to discuss these issues. They believe, and can cite examples to illustrate their beliefs, that the danger lies primarily in how Mr. Team would react. They simply do not believe that he would not get upset and would not hold such a discussion against them.

This is not the entire picture. Time and time again, I find that subordinates in such situations have as difficult problems with each other as each does with Mr. Team. In many cases, they would be relieved if they could work through these problems.

For example, I interviewed individually and as a team the immediate reports of Mr. Team. I found that they clearly understood what their Mr. Team espoused. They repeated individually and as a team every one of his concerns. For example, they said that he believed:

"The future is up to us as a team."

"Individually no one is strong enough to pull off the next innovation."

"We are not good at accepting anyone's leadership."

"We are a track team and not a basketball team. Mr. Team wants the latter."

The immediate reports, however, did not sense the depth of their boss's sadness and disappointment about the lack of a team. No one said, during the same sessions, words like "he's tired," "he's had it," "it really bewilders him."

Moreover, at least half of the immediate reports did not believe that the John Wayne metaphor was no longer valid. Indeed, many were waiting for the day when they would be heroes and ride off into the sunset. They also believed that it would be dangerous to express these different views. This expression could upset Mr. Team, and "if you upset him, you never know what will happen." Also, "you could appear unduly competitive with your peers."

Yet what is the evidence that it is dangerous to disagree on these issues? No one could give an example from their weekly staff meetings. One reason was that differences of this type were rarely discussed during these meetings.

When I met with the inner cabinet of Mr. Team's larger group, I became impressed with how ready they were to engage rather than bypass the problem of building a team. They wanted a session during which they could talk openly and constructively about the team issues with Mr. Team. What impressed me was that they wanted to make their own games and cover-ups a major item on the agenda. They had no interest in a session in which the problem was framed primarily as "the boss." They came prepared with suggestions of topics to be discussed and with concrete illustrations from the staff meetings.

The meeting was held. Mr. Team began by repeating that he wanted to build a team. In a moment of greater openness, however, he also said that he was reducing his level of aspiration about the team that could be produced and that he was getting tired of doing all the integrative work.

The cabinet members agreed with his concerns and gave illustrations from their own actions that made it difficult to build a team. They expanded the examples to include the larger group as well as several of Mr. Team's actions. Mr. Team confirmed the former examples but appeared to distance himself from examples describing his contributions. He said that he would not be a party to discussing these issues with his group because he thought that it would be destructive of human beings. He then gave an example of a private conversation that he intended to have with Mr. So-and-So in order to move him diplomatically out of the larger group in a way that no one would suspect Mr. So-and-So's failure.

Members of the subgroup were not surprised that Mr. Team felt that Mr. So-and-So was a poor performer. They were surprised and troubled because they felt that part of Mr. So-and-So's poor performance could be legitimately blamed on factors other than himself, including

Mr. Team. I was surprised that he would mention an individual by name before talking with that individual.

Mr. Team brought the meeting to a close by admitting that he was feeling agitated. He explained his emotional reactions as follows: It was the end of the week, and he was tired. He also said that the team issues were important and must be worked on. He invited his subgroup to meet with him and take the next step, but he ruled out discussions like these. The subgroup members agreed that confrontation could be harmful, but that was not what they had in mind. They had confidence that a session would lead to constructive consequences. Mr. Team disagreed.

The team members left the meeting feeling sad. Several said they had not predicted that Mr. Team would have become as uninfluenceable as he had become.

Summary of the Outcomes

Mr. Team Espoused	*Mr. Team Acted*
1. We must learn to work as a team. The era of the loner is gone.	1. I will decide by myself to reject the idea of a two-day session to discuss undiscussables that are barriers to team building.
2. We are all in control of the family jewels, especially people.	2. I will be in control, and you will give up the control whenever the discussion is not to my liking. (So much for the cabinet, which were his most cherished jewels.)
3. We must learn not to hold back and hedge when in a crunch.	3. I can hold back and hedge when in a crunch.
4. The culture has taught individuals not to be effective team members.	4. When my cabinet acts as an effective team in designing a workshop on team building with which I disagree, I will act as an individual and ignore the team.
5. Maybe executives like myself have been too soft on our subordinates.	5. I will be soft on myself and deny that this is what I am doing.
6. We must examine all the factors that inhibit the building of a team.	6. I will not permit the discussion of my fancy footwork.

Mr. Team explains the necessity of the existence of any inconsistencies on his part by saying, "I cannot permit discussions such as these because it might hurt them. I doubt that many of them can take it."

When I asked if such reasoning and action might not overprotect the individuals and inhibit building an effective team, Mr. Team sighed, smiled, and said, "As I told you, I may be too easy on them."

Fancy Footwork by a Subordinate

Fancy footwork is often associated with superiors over controlling subordinates, as was true in the previous case. The other side of the coin also happens, increasingly by young, very bright professionals such as consultants.

The young professionals whom I studied had excellent academic records. They had experienced few if any failures during undergraduate and graduate work. They had little experience with failure: their failure muscles were not very developed. Understandably, they feared failure; indeed, they even feared the experience of thinking about failure.

The same professionals were also highly motivated to perform excellent work. They were willing to work very hard, partially because it was their experience that hard work led to successful experiences. Another reason for their hard work was that they felt they were very well paid and therefore that their organization deserved to get their best performance.

This combination of a very high level of aspiration for success and an equally high level of fear of failure made the young professionals extremely vulnerable to making mistakes. Making a mistake led to feelings of excessive failure, and that, in turn, led to feelings of guilt. A metaphor often used by the young professionals to describe what they do when they make an error was doom zoom. The metaphor describes the feelings of doom as well as the pace in which those feelings arose—namely, very fast.

Not surprisingly, the young professionals fought being made responsible for errors. This was especially true with errors in dealing with people. Many of them had many success experiences in the classroom, where their primary relationship was with the instructor. They had learned how to be effective with their boss. Come prepared, do first-rate work, and show genuine interest and commitment to learning.

They had learned very little about dealing interdependently with their fellow students, however. Their major concerns were the instructor and their own performance. Most had been nurtured on the importance of excellent performance. Most sought the autonomy necessary to let them perform well. Most of them did not like being dependent on, or controlled by, other people. Most craved feedback about their performance, many fully expecting it to be positive. Consequently, most condemned the constricting features of a Model I world.

Their fancy footwork surfaced when they were given an opportunity to examine and change the barriers to their autonomy. For example, a group of young professionals criticized their superiors for giving them poor feedback on their performance, for not really caring or listening, and for distancing themselves from the career development issues that they as younger professionals faced. To the surprise of the professionals, the superiors recommended a study to get at the problems in order to correct them.

The professionals conducted the study with the assistance of an outsider, namely, myself. They designed and implemented a good study. Their analysis was sound. A one-day meeting was held to provide feedback to the top. The session was tape-recorded.

The bottom line was that the young professionals gave the feedback using exactly the same actions that they were complaining their supervisors used. For example, the professionals criticized superiors for being judgmental, unilateral, and abstract in their feedback. Yet, the professionals acted in the same way during their feedback session with the superiors. When the superiors struggled to get more concrete data or when they questioned the findings, in my opinion, in a constructive manner, the subordinates accused them of not "really" listening and of "becoming defensive." Not surprisingly, the subordinates soon distanced themselves from their superiors, thereby creating the very conditions that they condemned.

I intervened to point out these possibilities. The subordinates' initial reactions were that I was choosing sides and was no longer the neutral third party. I asked that we listen to a portion of the tape to test their attributions. After initial reluctance, they agreed to listen. The young professionals were surprised at and somewhat embarrassed by what they heard. They struggled to find evidence that their superiors' actions had caused their ineffective behavior. The tape confirmed their judgment in a few cases, but even those cases occurred after the subordinates had made their own presentation that was judgmental and abstract.

I was impressed with the defensiveness of the younger professionals once they felt that they were caught. They struggled to find causes of their ineffective behavior in the superior or the organization. I believe that without the tape recorder, it would have been difficult for them to accept that they were acting as counterproductively as they were accusing their superiors of acting. The tape recorder became the smoking gun that they could not deny.

To illustrate the depth of the fancy footwork that bright professionals can exhibit, I turn to another example. This one involves a vice-president (VP) in a consulting firm who was, in effect, trying to reduce organizational defensive routines in case teams in order to try out new ways to deliver services to the clients. He wanted to divide the tasks of the team according to disciplinary subjects. VP realized that structuring the case team this way would violate the norms. He therefore informed each of the young consultants about the experiment that he wished to try. He asked them to join him but emphasized that they should not do so if they were uncomfortable with the idea. The four consultants volunteered gladly. They liked the idea of being part of an experiment that might represent a new way of consulting.

VP told the young consultants that he was not concerned about their technical competence. He was concerned, however, about their ability to work interdependently. He said that he would try to make discussable any interpersonal issues that appeared to be getting in the way, even though typically they might not be discussable. The consultants responded that this made good sense.

Such a problem arose during an early case team meeting. VP said:

> VP: I should like to identify a problem and get your reactions.
> I asked you (Consultant 2) to get the information distributed. You said, "I already know it, so why should I do it?" This leads me to worry that for other issues, each individual may say, "I already know it. Why do I have to help the others?"
>
> CONS 1: In the spirit of the experiment, I should like to say that you are putting Consultant 2 on the spot unnecessarily. I think that you are taking a comment that he made with all good intentions and you're saying that there are all sorts of hidden agendas. I will be uncomfortable if we have to shift from professional problems to psychoanalysis.

Consultant 1 assumed that his view of what happened was correct. VP was placing Consultant 2 on the spot and was reading into the actions of other people intentions that were not there. He also placed the VP on notice that he would not cooperate with the emphasis on "psychoanalysis." Consultant 1 assumed that his diagnosis was correct, that the problem was VP's action. Consultant 1 did not encourage inquiry into his own views. He intimated that further discussions like these would make him and the others uncomfortable. This attitude placed VP in a dilemma because if he wanted to inquire into Consultant 1's views and feelings, Consultant 1 could respond, "There you go again, getting clinical."

In another episode VP raised another concern. He acknowledged that he was prone to making sweeping statements. He wanted his and others' statements confronted.

> VP: I'm worried that if I agree with something, it may be taken as final. Also, it is important for me to be able to say, "Hold on, I think it is more complicated than that," without suppressing others' views or being seen as unfair.

Cons 1: I would say that you are being unnecessarily nervous about this case team.

Again, we see the pattern of Consultant 1's holding the VP responsible and psychoanalyzing him ("you are being unnecessarily nervous") even though he would not want others to psychoanalyze him.

Later, the VP attempted to question Consultant 1 on his style of dealing with a technical problem. VP preferred to examine a lot of data from which to develop insights. Consultant 1 tended to ignore data and to focus on "getting the big picture," which meant that he focused on concepts and theory first and later looked for supporting data. VP was concerned that early theorizing could lead to missing the complexity of the situation or could lead the team to see primarily what their framing told them to see. He was especially worried about these possibilities because the experiment was to try to understand the problem as it existed for the client. Too often theories were discipline-centered. The VP then gave an example of Consultant 1's speculations, which seemed not to fit the client. Also, if Consultant 1 had looked at the data available, he would see that they did not confirm his ideas.

VP: As I see it, you talk as if your idea is correct. I can't see the evidence for it. I know that I don't know the answer. Your reaction appears to be, "that is my problem."

Cons 1: No. I'm saying there are two different views with two different implications. You're saying my idea is not a useful construct. Besides, since you have the data, you have the right answer. So why the hell am I speculating.

VP was accused of saying that he had the answer, which was the opposite of his position. VP wanted Consultant 1 to speculate but to test his speculations earlier with the data. Consultant 1 became upset and suggested that he might withdraw from the case team.

VP: My problem is why do I have to pursue every speculative line of argument you come up with before you have examined the data available? Why not test your speculations?

Cons 1: OK. Why don't I waste our time with pursuing speculations.

VP: No. Tell me why I should listen. I'm willing to do so if there is good reason.

Cons 1: No. You're right, you're right. There's no good in my speculations.

Instead of Consultant 1's exploring why VP might find it useful to explore Consultant 1's speculations, he responded by asserting that VP was accusing him of wasting the team's time and insisting that he was correct. VP denied that he was saying these things. Instead of Consultant 1's exploring with VP the differences in views in order to help VP see his possible blind spots, Consultant 1 jumped to the conclusions that VP was correct and that his own nonspeculations were wrong. The only way these conclusions could be correct was if one followed the logic embedded in Consultant 1's argument. Moreover, his assertions that VP was correct and that Consultant 1 was wrong were tantamount to saying that he adhered to logic that he was willing to denounce.

Later, VP challenged Consultant 1's speculations with the use of some data already collected by the other team members.

> CONS 1: OK. There you go again. You are suppressing people's desire to discuss speculation by shooting them down with data.
>
> I made a speculation, and you said, "That's not right because ___," and you gave the data. Final word! Bang! I've spoken. I know more about it than you do. Stop!
>
> VP: What I hear you saying essentially is, "I'm speculating, and you start to raise questions that squelch my speculations."
>
> Don't we have the right to confront yours, and all our reasoning?
>
> CONS 1: OK. I don't agree. But to make my point, I would have to speculate. That would consume more of our time, so let's drop it.
>
> VP: Well, I would rather not. I would rather that you help me to see if and where I'm wrong. It doesn't make sense for me to ask you to be confrontable on your ideas, and I should not be.

The fancy footwork pattern is similar to the one we saw earlier used by Mr. Team. Consultant 1 made attributions about VP that he never tested publicly. He used self-sealing logic to prove that his own view was correct. Unlike the previous situation, however, the individual producing the fancy footwork was encouraged to express his views and to examine not only his actions but also those of VP. The first difference, therefore, was that fancy footwork was made discussable. The second difference was that Consultant 1 did not have the power to require VP to withdraw. Therefore, Consultant 1 threatened to withdraw. This strategy is based on the assumption that one way to threaten VP is to suggest that, if he continued, the case team and the client would lose the services of a first-rate technical mind.

In other words, Mr. Team and VP espoused similar values. We must learn to work together as a team. The era of the loner is gone. We are all in control of our precious assets. We must learn not to hold back and hedge. We must examine all the factors that inhibit the building of a team. In this case, however, it was the subordinate who acted in ways that rewarded being a loner, seeking unilateral control, hedging and fighting interdependence, and denying or sweeping under the rug actions that inhibited the building of an effective team. Fancy footwork, therefore, closed off learning for the VP, for both players, and for the other team members who observed the win/lose dynamics.

Consultant 1 placed VP in a double bind. If VP confronted errors that were embarrassing or threatening, Consultant 1 might go into a doom zoom and blame him for being inhumane. If VP did not confront the errors, the quality of the service could be reduced.

Officers deal with this bind by trying to select consultants who are reputed to have less powerful doom zooms, by easing in on the issues, and by minimizing interdependence and public discussions of the quality of the team as a team. If there is a serious problem, team members will deal with it individually. This approach saves face for everyone. It also permits the young consultants to tell their peers stories of what happened that are magnified in their favor. This is another defensive routine that enables the young consultants to maintain their feelings of failure at a minimum. Sometimes these stories get back to the officers, usually in their magnified form, which angers them. In their minds, however, to engage these defensive routines will make the illness worse.

The irony is that these organizational defensive routines become taken for granted. They are lamented by all players but accepted as part of organizational life. Once the defensive routines take hold, they, in turn, take hold of the players. The players feel helpless about changing them. For the brittle consultants, that may not be all bad, because they can feel that their fancy footwork is predictable and understandable by all others. For the officers, they may conclude that distancing themselves from the consultants on issues that may be embarrassing or threatening is necessary—indeed, that it is a sign of caring.

I have an ending to tell about this example that came to me quite by accident. Consultant 1, I knew, had left the firm in which I had studied his actions in order to start his own firm. For several years he was quite successful.

During a plane trip, I sat next to an individual who worked in the new firm. As we spoke, I learned that the new firm was in trouble. The biggest problem, according to my seatmate, was the "arrogant" behavior of Consultant 1, especially toward the customers. He told me that he quit the organization not because of the arrogance per se but because, in his opinion, Consultant 1 was blind to his arrogance and closed to changing it.

I agreed that Consultant 1 was closed to learning. I did not, however, tell my informant that I did not agree that Consultant 1 was blind. My mind flashed back (privately) to the episode when I had asked Consultant 1 to give me his reaction to the total transcript from which this case was written. He told me that he had read it, that he felt embarrassed, and that he did not wish to talk about it any further.

I responded that it was up to him to choose how he would react. I also suggested that he consider that if his behavior was so upsetting that he wanted to forget it, someday the same behavior might be so painful to other people that they might act in the same way toward him.

Fancy Footwork by a Group

This story is about ten senior organizational development professionals and line personnel managers. They had participated in an educational program to become more effective in planning and producing educational change programs to engage and reduce skilled incompetence and organizational defensive routines.

They attended a one-week workshop in which they learned to diagnose how often, unawares, they helped create the defensive routines they decried. They learned how they produced actions that they themselves were advising other people not to produce. Although many found the diagnostic activities to be at times painful and embarrassing, they all reported to their superiors that they wished to continue the learning experience by meeting one day a month for a year. The superiors, after careful questioning, agreed to support the second phase.

The second phase was designed to teach the participants how to produce the new skills under everyday working conditions. The episode in question is about two members who had developed a plan for a three-day workshop on a subject requested by top line management. They presented the memo to the group and asked for a candid critique.

Several participants began by saying that they thought the two professionals had serious doubts about the entire project. Yet they had not discussed these doubts with their clients (several senior line managers). One colleague asked a series of questions. She ended her inquiry with, "You mean that you have designed a workshop about something you don't believe?" The two answered yes; they had had to do so because they were under pressure from line to present something immediately.

I expressed two concerns. First, that the two professionals were permitting themselves to be coerced into designing workshops that they believed were inappropriate. Second, if this pattern continued, their organization would not be well served, and they would probably build up angry and hostile feelings toward the line executives that, in turn, could reduce their own effectiveness.

I recommended that the organizational development professionals discuss their views with the executives in order to reverse the coercive relationship and in order to alter the design. I then continued:

> For the two to tell us that they're uncomfortable and blame the clients is inadequate. They tell us that they are concerned about the unfair actions of the line, but they did not analyze their own feelings. They blame the line mangement for overloading them. But maybe we can help them to figure out how they got themselves into this bind.

Another member asked me, "Are you saying, in effect, that their memorandum was incompetent?" I said yes.

One writer became openly upset with my response. The other did not, but he did feel badly. I asked that we reflect on the episode and examine what we had said and done.

One author of the memorandum and several members of the workshop began by saying that I had evaluated the memorandum negatively, that I did not show support for the effort that had gone into it. I agreed that I had evaluated the memorandum negatively. I also agreed that I did not support their blaming the clients for their product. I did not want to collude in that strategy.

The conversation that they produced contained the unrecognized gaps and inconsistencies similar to the cases described earlier.

They Said	*What the Transcript Showed*
1. You could have used another term. *Incompetent* is too harsh.	1. One of their peers used the term. I confirmed it. When I asked them to role-play how they would say it, they all eased in. Their own peers experienced them as covering up and being manipulative.
2. You could have said something positive first, and then the negative. For example, "It is clear that you two struggled hard and you've gotten this far. Now here's what I see that isn't working."	2. I could not reward their hard work because the authors admitted that because they were swamped and overworked, they spent only several hours on the report. I wanted to help them deal with the deeper problem of their going along with being continually swamped by their clients, because that was a recipe for never having enough time to do the job right. I also reminded them that all of them had complained of being overworked and swamped.

They Said	*What the Transcript Showed*
3. Say something positive first, so that the person can concentrate on those parts that are at issue.	3. When asked to role-play an example, the individuals who made the recommendation could not. "It depends on the situation," they said. When encouraged to focus on the situation that they all had experienced in the group, or on any other situation, both said they wanted to think about it.

After several hours of discussion, we attempted to develop a map of the defensive routines being used in the session. The map looked like this:

If negatively evaluated ——→ we feel ——→ hurt and scared.

Some of the reasons that we feel this way are:

1. Maybe we cannot produce the behavior that we value and that we advise others to produce.
2. We were wrong; it appeared to be unaware.
3. We feel a sense of failure.
4. We feel shame and guilt.

We React by Asserting:	
The evaluator is unfair, judgmental, harsh.	If evaluator presents valid data to illustrate why he does not feel that he was unfair and why he was unconflicted about being judgmental, then go to the next response.
We are overloaded; overload is unfair.	If evaluator agrees that we are overloaded and wishes to help us, but wants to begin with our contribution to the problem, then respond by saying . . .
You are unrealistic. The schedule cannot be changed. The superiors are not influenceable.	If evaluator says that these evaluations and attributions of the superiors might be tested, otherwise they are doing to their superiors what they rejected of the evaluator (i.e., being judgmental and harsh).
You are unrealistic. You try it. I won't. I could disappear.	

The fancy footwork characteristics involved were to:

1. Assert that I acted in ways that were not supportive (Model I view of support).
2. Assert that I could have acted more effectively. When asked to illustrate the other way, the individual was unable to produce it.
3. Assert that I acted in ways that, the transcript shows, I did not.
4. Go to a new series of causes that are beyond the control of the group when the causes they establish appear to be invalidated.
5. Assert that the problems are unsolvable.

This map, the group members agreed, represented not only the reactions of many people in the group; it also represented how many other human resources professionals would act if their reasoning or actions were questioned seriously, even though they might have asked for a tough critique. The professionals felt that many individuals withhold candid criticism because they believe that such criticism would set off a chain reaction such as this and that they would end up in the doghouse.

Organizational Malaise

Fancy footwork is not cost-free to the organization. If all the players are using it, then the inconsistencies, dodging, and blindness to one's own involvement in it all become a part of fabric of the organizational culture. The features of this fancy footwork form a pattern that is easy to see and experience but difficult to grab hold of in order to reduce. People feel and sense a disease from experiencing it, but they feel helpless to alter it. This is why one thoughtful human resources vice-president called it *malaise.*

Symptoms of organizational malaise were (1) seeking and finding fault with the organization but not accepting responsibility for correcting it, (2) accentuating the negative and deemphasizing the positive, and (3) espousing values that everyone knows are not implementable but acting as if they are.

Fault the Organization and Do Not Feel Responsible for Correcting the Faults

People fault the organization and blame others or the system for the faults. They do not take responsibility for creating the faults or for correcting them.

For example, an organization had just completed a massive organizational diagnosis. A corporate committee was set up to make sense of the results. The committee worked diligently to identify some organizational defensive routines that they believed the top used. These defenses not only made the top less effective but also made it easier for the poor performers at the lower levels to hide in safety.

The committee spent several hours deciding what they should write in their report to the top. They concluded that it was the better part of valor to water down their analysis because the top was too brittle to respond constructively. Needless to say, they never tested this attribution about the top with the top. Nor did they explore how often individuals took this stance vis-à-vis management, thereby holding them responsible for the fault.

Accentuate the Negative and Deemphasize the Positive

Individuals not only see the faults in the organization; they also magnify them. One reason they magnify the faults is that the more powerful and awesome they can make the faults seem, the easier it is for the individuals to explain away their own distancing and feelings of helplessness.

Individuals under these conditions often discuss the faults with a sense of pleasure because finding them reassures individuals that their distancing and helplessness are necessary.

At times some individuals may say that they are tired of all the negativity. In their opinion, the organization is a fine firm, and people should stand up for it. The plea is usually made with a good deal of passion. It is usually followed by other people being silent or expressing mild agreement. The most powerful consequence, however, is that expressing the complaint is also being negative. Therefore, the complaint can be downplayed, if not ignored.

These rules of fancy footwork tell people to criticize the organization and downplay its positive features. They tell people it is their responsibility to find fault with the organization but not to feel personally responsible for correcting it. The rules encourage people to be realistic by distancing themselves from trying to generate major changes in the organizational defensive routines.

People Espouse Values That They Cannot Implement

In organizations that are genuinely concerned with people, individuals find themselves in a dilemma because they espouse values that are difficult to implement in the face of the organizational defense routines and fancy footwork.

For example, in one forward-looking organization, the CEO often espoused the values in the left-hand column below, yet he and other people acknowledged that the activities in the right-hand column continued to exist without much diminution.

Values Espoused		*Activities*
Excellence	yet	mediocrity rises to the top unless it is continually beaten back by top management.
Employee involvement and commitment	yet	when it comes to the tough decisions and issues, many of the employees distance themselves from being responsible for the inconsistencies and mediocre performance.
Cooperation among groups or departments	yet	there exist coalition groups and interdepartmental warfare that produce politics and rivalries that protect turf and key individuals' egos.

Under these conditions, people will behave consistently with the right-hand column and yet will espouse the values in the left-hand column. This is equivalent to making the values a fad and eventually not credible. Individuals will also resist examining the defensive reasoning in their fancy footwork that helps to produce the problem in the first place. For example, an individual might say:

1. I value excellence, yet mediocrity exists.
2. I deal with this inconsistency by using fancy footwork, some of which I am aware of and some of which I am not.

   The fancy footwork of which I am aware is to blame mediocrity on others, on the organizational culture, or on the larger culture. The fancy footwork of which I am not aware is how infrequently I confront my and others' distancing from doing anything about the discrepancy except to emphasize excellence.
3. By using the emphasis on excellence as a way to deal with mediocrity, coupled with distancing from confronting the causes of the mediocrity (among which is their own fancy footwork), I, in effect, make a promise that I cannot keep. The promise is to fight for excellence. The reason I cannot keep it is my own and others' fancy footwork, which also makes it difficult for me to see how I reinforce mediocrity.

4. Because I am unaware of my own responsibility, I revert to blaming others or the organization.

The result is that blaming others in the organization makes it possible for individuals to feel in control by acting in ways that create organizational malaise and their being out of control. The inconsistencies caused by the malaise are designed by their own self-protected inconsistencies.

Conclusion: The Organizational Defense Pattern (ODP)

All organizations contain, in varying amounts, skilled incompetence, organizational defensive routines, organizational fancy footwork, and the consequences that flow from these. They form a pattern, an organizational defensive pattern (ODP). ODP is generic to all human organizations, including private and public organizations, trade unions, voluntary organizations, universities and schools, as well as families (see Figure 4.1).

ODP results from individuals' coping with embarrassment or threat. Organizations are not the original cause of ODP. It is caused by the theory-in-use and social virtues most individuals learn during their early years. They combine to create skilled incompetence, which, in turn, creates organizational defensive routines, fancy footwork, and malaise. They all coexist and reinforce each other. Thus, once in existence, they make up the ODP.

What prevents the ODP from causing blowups?

- *Not all errors involve embarrassment or threat. There is a lot of work that gets done well; goals are achieved.*
- *Management works hard at reducing the causes of embarrassment or threat by creating sound organizational structures and policies. Management also creates programs or visions toward excellence that, in theory, can be used to counteract the rigidity, hopelessness, and cynicism of the organizational defensive routines.*
- *The very act of driving the pattern underground reduces the likelihood of blowing things up. People work hard not to open up Pandora's box; they learn to be skillful at working through organizational mine fields.*
- *People become desensitized over time even to recognizing or feeling embarrassed or threatened by withdrawing or distancing themselves. They develop a low sense of personal responsibility for the pattern. If they accept that they activate the pattern, they usually do so because they hold someone else or the system responsible.*

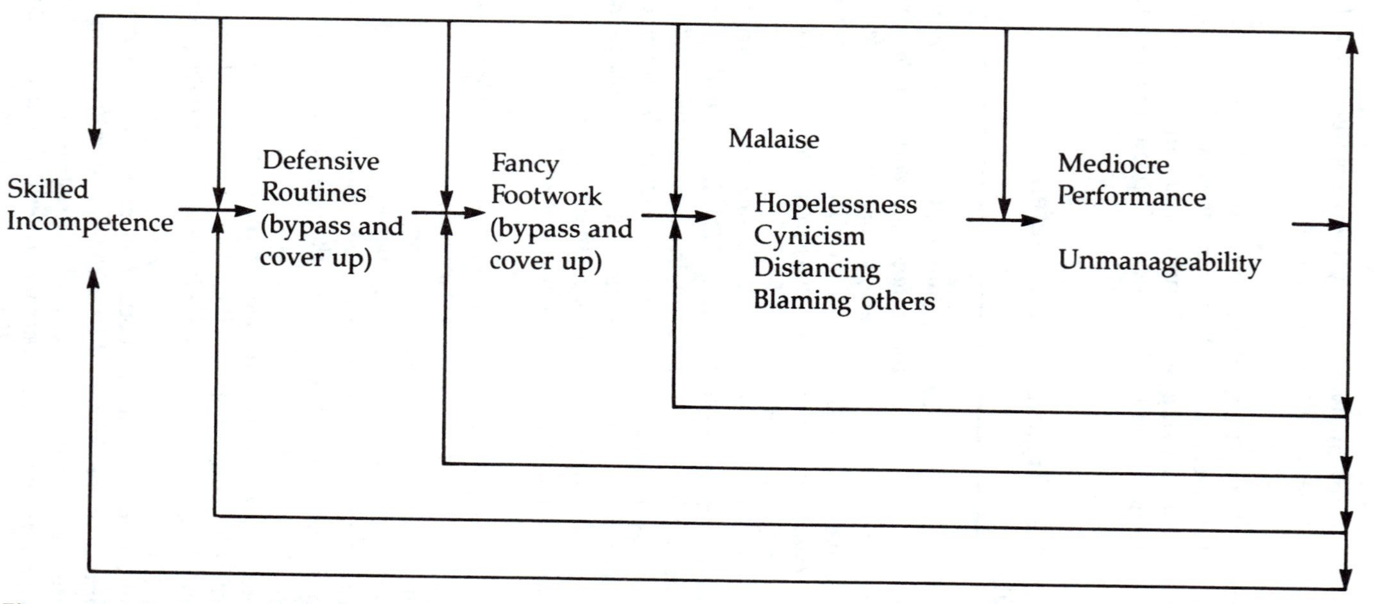

Figure 4.1 ***Organizational Defensive Pattern***

- *People who are committed and highly involved and who feel personally responsible will eventually become tired, exhausted, and burned out. The pattern hurts people who care deeply for the organization's health. People who have withdrawn use the pattern to protect themselves by holding the pattern responsible for their own defensive activities.*
- *People do leave, especially those who care and become exhausted. For example, they take other jobs or early retirement, they leave to create new organizations, or they become one-person organizations and consult. The irony is that the solution is a temporary one for the individual (because even small organizations develop the pattern). It is a loss for the original organization, which loses some of its best people.*
- *Finally, there are blowups at the organizational and individual levels. In the case of the former, an organization may no longer be efficient and effective, partially due to the rigidities created by the organizational defensive pattern. In the case of the latter, many people do experience a feeling of burnout. There may be thousands of individual blowups that are dealt with by human beings' leaving, seeking psychological help, being transferred to less demanding jobs, or withdrawing into self-protective shells.*

I believe that the constructive actions for minimizing organizational blowups, such as programs for excellence, are inherently less powerful than is the organizational defensive pattern. One reason is that the pattern exists and flourishes without formal organizational support. It has to be strong to survive. A second reason is that the programs for excellence are designed to bypass features of the organizational defensive pattern. Every bypass is an act of recognition of the defensive pattern and simultaneously an act of its power. It is so powerful that it should be bypassed. Thus, every bypass strengthens the organizational defensive pattern.

Prologue to Action

Two fundamental strategies can be used to reduce the ODP activities that create and legitimize error. The first strategy is to design and manage organizations in ways that do not activate the organizational defensive pattern in the first place. These ways, in effect, act to reduce errors that are likely to be embarrassing or threatening. Examples are the redesign of work, autonomous groups, and other features of the new theories of employee involvement. The assumption is that these new organizational features tap individuals' capabilities and competences in such a way that these individuals can be more effective performers with little management from superiors.

Since these new ideas are built on human capabilities and competences, it is possible to teach the new skills and actions required because people have the potential to learn. The changes are based on using their known potentials. This means that massive reeducation and change programs are feasible because the new organizational features can be packaged into legitimate requirements, such as new job descriptions and new management responsibilities, many of which are assigned to employees.

As we see in the next chapter, implementing the new theory of management is full of challenges that can be, at times, embarrassing and threatening to some management and employees. Because they have not been taught how to reduce their skilled incompetence and the organizational defensive routines and fancy footwork, the managers or employees will activate them when facing embarrassment or threat.

Both sides will see such reactions as betrayals of the new philosophy of management. Both will be correct. The old theory of management is consistent with Model I theory-in-use. The new theory of management is consistent with Model II theory-in-use, described in chapter 6. The point now is that these two theories-in-use are based on different values and require different skills.

The second strategy is to educate individuals with new concepts and skills that engage the features of the organizational defensive pattern in such a way as to reduce them. The strategy is not to bypass and cover up but to engage and make discussable and manageable. As individuals use the new skills, they begin to change the organizational defensive routines and fancy footwork. As that begins to happen, new concepts of control, especially related to budgets, management information systems, and employee rewards, can be introduced. Imagine a budget or a financial resource allocations process based on trust!

The next chapter describes the important changes many organizations are implementing in work design and management of work groups. This emphasis on managing through involvement is showing some striking results when implemented correctly. The chapter begins by describing the underlying reasons these programs can be expected to work. It closes by examining how getting from here to there, and indeed the very success of these programs, can lead to embarrassment and threat, which will require strategy two to be implemented.

The two strategies are highly interdependent. They can be implemented simultaneously. Experience to date shows that if an organization begins with the first strategy at the lower levels, then it should begin with the second strategy immediately, if not beforehand, at the upper levels.

Reference

Baum, Howell S. 1987. *The Invisible Bureaucracy.* New York: Oxford University Press.

Chapter Five

Sound Advice: It Compounds the Problem

▸ What if the executives wanted to begin to reduce the organizational defensive routines, fancy footwork, and malaise in their organizations? What if they read the advice that comes from the best and the brightest? If they took this advice seriously, they would get into trouble.

Why? Because the overwhelming amount of the advice does not deal directly with these factors. Most of the people offering advice act as if these problems did not exist. Or, where the problems are acknowledged to exist, the advice given to reduce, for example, the organizational defensive routines would actually strengthen them. Or the advice is so abstract that it is difficult to use to take action, yet it is written as if this is not the case.

For example, Thomas Horton (1986) selected sixteen chief executives because of their successful records as change agents, as "movers and shakers." These leaders exhibited the ultimate quality of leadership, a quality James MacGregor Burns (1978) called the ability to transform, to be transforming leaders.

As far as I could see, many of these successful leaders tacitly recognized the existence of organizational defensive routines, fancy footwork, and malaise. But their advice gives us little insight into how to behave. The advice is at a high level of inference and is not operational, a central characteristic of the MacGregor Burns book.

The leadership books, of which quite a few have been published in recent years, all have the same important limitations. They focus on espoused theories. They do not provide the data needed to understand the theory-in-use.

Consider these examples from Henry B. Schacht of Cummins Engine:[1]

States	*Leaves Unspecified*
"I know only that we had good people and a discipline to approach the situation, plus a high degree of good humor and a good sense of our own fallibility."	What are the characteristics of "good people"? What are the features of a "disciplined approach" and a "good sense of our own fallibility"? How would one recognize them?
"We work very hard at a sense of collective responsibility and collective performance. But that doesn't mean there isn't individual responsibility within that.	How to produce collective responsibility and collective performance under conditions of embarrassment or threat.
[One] must blend the individual sense of accountability within a general sense of sharing."	How to produce the blend, especially when the forces are against it.

James Burke, CEO of Johnson and Johnson, advises:[2]

"It's only natural for people to want to tell me how things are going at the moment, but I tell them to talk about the future."	How does he divert them from the natural to doing something less natural? Why is it less natural in the first place? How do they react to him? Are they upset? Do they cover up? Does it make any difference to Burke? If so, how does he deal with it?
"I don't think it bruises people to argue and debate. You'd be surprised how easy some of our young people find it to politely say, 'You know, you're wrong; . . . you don't have the facts . . . I do, and here's the evidence to prove it.' "	How do they talk politely, and not bruise, when they talk about other people's defensive routines and fancy footwork? How do they encourage confrontation of their own views if this is what they say? What is the impact on the problem-solving process if there are individuals who find this model approach counterproductive?

1. All quotations are from Horton (1986), p. 286.
2. All quotations are from Horton (1986), p. 15.

Frank T. Cary, CEO of IBM, advises:[3]

"I learned the technique of intense questioning. When someone came and started to make a presentation, I would stop them at the outset." (p. 202)	How does he produce intense questioning without making people intense? If it is all right for them to become intense, how does he deal with these feelings? How does he recognize them if they choose to cover up? How would he stop them? What would he say?
"I'd ask, 'What is it that you're recommending?' I made them explain in a way that was meaningful." (p. 202)	How does he recognize a meaningful way from a nonmeaningful way? How does he act to make them explain in a meaningful way? Why do executives explain issues in nonmeaningful ways in the first place? Are they unaware of doing so? If so, why?
"All IBM managers are motivated to do a job; one of IBM's great strengths. The trick is a matter of knowing how to set the agenda . . . to get people working together." (p. 203)	What does he actually say, and how does he act to set the agenda to get people working together? Why do they need someone to set the agenda if they are motivated to do a good job? Why don't they set the agenda the way he would?
"When he was in charge of corporate staff he encouraged them to operate in a contention mode. When he became general manager of the data processing group, he changed his agenda to eliminating contention and conflict." (p. 203)	What did he say and do to encourage contention? What did he say and do to discourage contention? Any ideas of why he needed to do this in the first place?

Peter Drucker, one of the world's premier authors on management, writes (1973):[4]

"Organizitis," self-inflicted hypochondria, should be avoided.	How would other people identify "organizitis" and hypochondria? How can someone avoid them if they are inflicting them on their organization? How do they overcome the skilled unawareness that is required to implement the advice?

3. All quotations are from Horton (1986).
4. All quotations are from Drucker (1973).

"Organizational change should not be taken often and should not be undertaken lightly. . . . A certain amount of friction, of incongruity, or organizational confusion is inevitable." (p. 549).	What criteria can be used to specify what is taken often and what is taken lightly? How much of the inevitable friction, incongruity, and confusion is acceptable? When does it become unacceptable? How can you tell before that happens?
"One can either work or meet. One cannot do both at the same time." (p. 403)	Why is it not possible to create problem-solving processes that combine meetings with work?
"The only thing that is proven by a man's not performing in a given assignment is that management made a mistake by putting him in." (p. 457)	Why did management make a mistake about which it was unaware? Does management carry some of the blame? How would managers know when the advice is not self-sealing their own limits?

To summarize, the advice the executives give is abstract and disconnected from telling the reader what behavior is required to implement it. If people talk about the present, get them to talk about the future. If people make presentations in nonmeaningful ways, get them to make their presentations in meaningful ways. If people lack a disciplined approach, get them to be more disciplined.

Nor do the advice givers seem to make distinctions between errors that are due to ignorance and those that are designed. It is one kind of problem if senior executives do not make meaningful presentations, ignore the future, and are not disciplined in their problem solving because they are unaware of what is a meaningful presentation, of focusing on the future, and of being disciplined. If these problems exist, then one could wonder why these individuals became senior executives reporting to such chief executive officers.

What if (and I believe this is more likely) the errors are designed? Then the advisors miss recommending to the reader how to separate undesigned from designed error. They also do not tell the reader how to find out what causes executives to produce designed errors, how such errors are covered up, or to what extent the culture and the actions of the executives coerce designed errors.

True, all the advice is abstract. But that is not the main problem. All advice will be communicated with abstractions. That is the way the mind works when it is crafting advice. The key is to connect the abstractions unambiguously with actual behavior. For example, advice as to how to produce a good sense of personal fallibility, or how to create a sense of collective responsibility, or how to divert people from the wrong behavior to the correct behavior is abstract. The questions are, What are the actual words to be used? How would these words be crafted?

Without the words, the recipient has no tangible feel of the advice. Without the words, the advice will, in all likelihood, be produced consistently with Model I. If that happens, the advice will not only be counterproductive, it will also make its user be seen by other people as being inconsistent and unaware of the inconsistency.

Some readers may wonder if it is fair to use the previous quotations to build the argument. After all, the executives might do what I am suggesting. However, I doubt that this is true for most of them. First, I have worked with many executives such as these, and they rarely illustrate their advice. They craft their advice pretty much as they are quoted here.

True, when asked, many are willing to exemplify by simulating what they would actually say. In most cases, however, when I ask them to analyze the theory-in-use in the conversation that they crafted, it is almost always consistent with Model I. Yet the advice they gave would be productive if it were not crafted consistently with Model I. These executives, as is true of those described in chapter 2, all felt stuck. The irony is that if readers try to implement their advice, they, too, would get stuck, but they would be unaware of how counterproductive their actions were to the recipients.

There is a second reason I believe using these quotations is fair. Editors like Horton are well-known professionals with excellent reputations, as are their publishers. Both know the norms about what to communicate and what sells. Thus, they are following the ideas in good currency about how to communicate advice effectively. These norms that make it possible to disconnect abstractions from behavior are predictable if human beings use Model I theory-in-use and if the people are embedded in organizational defensive patterns.

Advice That Reinforces Designed Errors and Organizational Defensive Routines

The second feature of the advice given in the literature is that it reinforces the organizational defensive pattern. For example:

Reginald Jones of General Electric periodically sought honest feedback from his immediate subordinates. His practice was to assign an executive whom everyone trusted to chair the meeting. That executive would give Jones the feedback without violating any confidence (Mills 1985).

The premise on which this strategy is based is that individual and organizational defensive routines are so strong that subordinates cannot level with their superiors, especially when the issues may contain embarrassing or threatening information. This premise makes sense in a world of skilled incompetence and defensive routines.

However, Jones never tests the validity of the premise with the subordinates. He covers up his attributions and acts as if he is not covering up. His subordinates interpret this action as an indication of concern for the human side of the enterprise. I too believe that Jones had these intentions. I also believe that strategies like these are likely to make the present problems self-fulfilling and the counterproductive reasoning self-sealing.

James R. Martin, CEO of Massachusetts Mutual Life Insurance Company, tells how hard he tried to receive bad news from below as early as possible. He formed an Executive Council. He persuaded members of the council to go off by themselves twice a year for a one- or two-day meeting. He proposed these sessions to be a risk-free opportunity for members to criticize him and the way he worked. Following each meeting, one member would report back the group findings. The meetings inevitably began with the group representative saying, "Of course, Jim, these don't necessarily represent my views, but the group feels that you should . . . ." Martin found the feedback valuable (Horton 1986, 113).

Martin, like Jones, had created a structure that encouraged openness and simultaneously bypassed the organizational defensive routines that would prevent that openness with him present in the first place.

Recently Bruce (1986) interviewed fourteen retired successful CEOs of large corporations on issues of leadership. Trust was a key factor:

> "I worked with a man . . . who often confided in me how lousy he thought one of my associates was. I found myself wondering what he was saying about me to that associate. Every relationship must have the solid foundation of trust if it is to withstand the eroding waves of daily happenings." (Bruce 1986, 5)

The CEO mistrusted the colleague but never told him so; indeed, he covered up his feelings of mistrust. Every act of cover-up erodes the trust. Thus, the CEO was also responsible for eroding trust, but in his case, he would say he was doing so in the name of concern and caring.

> "[My] former CEO was usually a very easy person to talk to, but periodically he would don the mantle of the office, and at that point I would back off and start putting the information through channels. Once you do that, the information gets filtered." (Bruce 1986, 7)

The author writes, "to this I added a silent amen."

Here, we have a CEO describing conditions under which he colluded to create information distortion because, he reasoned, his ex-superior's actions required it. The attribution was never tested with the individual involved. The reasoning for the response, which the CEO describes as counterproductive, was covered up and kept silent. The author automatically empathized with the requirement for silence; he wrote that he added a silent "amen."

> "The CEO is the leader, he sets the tone and the direction of the organization.
>
> "Suddenly you [CEO] are faced with the realization . . . I'm here and there is nobody else.
>
> "My job was to keep people focused on getting the job done by cajoling, wheeling, and constantly keeping the pressure on. In the end, it was rewarding to get where you wanted and to have everyone with you."

As far as the defensive tone of organizations, the leader is never alone. His colleagues are colluding with him. The tone does not get set only by what the CEO does but also by how the subordinates choose to react. Most subordinates would choose to react the way the CEOs suggest, because they are all programmed in the same ways.

The reason the CEO feels alone is *not* because there is nobody else but because he and the others act in ways that result in his becoming distant. For example, the logic that in order to be objective with regard to personnel decisions the CEO must maintain a degree of aloofness is a self-fulfilling prophecy. The assertion that aloofness is the only way to gain objectivity may be true for the world as it is, but it is also self-reinforcing and self-sealing. The irony is that the aloofness may be reciprocated by subordinates. Their way of being aloof is not to distance themselves because that would be open. Rather, the subordinates may act in ways that they believe the superior prefers and hide that this is not their own preference. In the end, aloofness breeds further aloofness, and both breed distorted data that the CEO deals with objectively.

Burke (Horton 1986) noted that he found "a great deal of disagreement and anger about how bureaucratic we'd become here at headquarters [Johnson & Johnson]" (p. 27). Yet nobody there had been aware of it. His solution was to have meetings, at least once every three years, to examine these issues. He did not, as far as I could tell, ask the line participants why they withheld their views for so long. What skills did headquarters people have that made them blind and unaware?

Bellesario (Horton 1986) tells that she found that ten people would take 203 days to write up the minutes of the meetings. She dug into the problem and found all sorts of bureaucratic defensive routines that caused this inefficiency. Solution: She stipulated either no minutes of the meetings or one person prepare them. The result was that the ten people agreed to one person's writing up the minutes. Bellesario, however, never asked these people to explore the causes of the organizational defensive routines that had led them to take these unproductive steps. The subordinates distanced themselves from their responsibility by working unproductively. She stopped the unproductive action but maintained the distancing from their personal responsibility because she was responsible for the change.

Anthony and Young (1984) offer advice on how to deal with budget games. All the responses are consistent with Model I, organizational defensive routines, and fancy footwork.

For example, in dealing with the divide-and-conquer ploy, the authors recommend, "Responsibilities should be clearly defined, but this is easier said than done" (p. 377). Or, in dealing with distraction, they advise "Expose the hidden aims, but this is very difficult" (p. 378).

In dealing with the ploy of nothing is too good for our people, the recommendation is "Attempt to shift the discussion from emotional grounds to logical grounds by analyzing the request to see if the benefits are even remotely related to cost. Emphasize that in a world of scarce resources, not everyone can get all that is deserved" (p. 380).

Assume for the moment that people who use the ploy are relatively sophisticated bureaucratic infighters, an assumption that seems valid because they know enough to use the ploy. I guess that these people are prepared to defend their proposal as definitely being related to costs. They may even feel insulted to hear someone use the argument that in a world of scarce human resources, not all people can get what they deserve. They know this is true, and that is why they are pushing hard and using the ploys. The way the shift is made from the emotional to the logical could result in escalating emotions.

If the individuals use misleading but appealing labels, "look behind the euphemism to the real functions. If the disguise is intentional, deny the request, and if feasible, discourage recurrence by special punishment" (p. 381). Another possibility is to ask the individuals to examine the reasoning behind their actions. For example, "What leads you to believe that you must use misleading labels with us?" This line of reasoning could begin to uncover the defensive routines in place.

Frederick R. Kappel, when he was the CEO of AT&T, identified six danger signs of inbred management. They occur when:

1. People cling to old ways of working even though they have been confronted by a new situation.
2. They fail to define new goals with meaning and challenge.
3. Action is taken without studied reflection.
4. Institutionalized contentment exists: Business becomes secure and stable, not venturesome.
5. Old "wisdom" is passed on to new people. Older managers tend to adhere too rigidly to old ideas, to antiquated approaches and methods.
6. Low tolerance for criticism acts to stifle independent thinking.

This list makes sense. People do cling to their old ways, they do pass on "old" wisdom, and so on. Indeed, all these actions are predictable consequences of the organizational defensive pattern. Yet Kappel does not discuss such factors or how to overcome them.

Structural Advice Is Preferable to Behavioral Advice

The third feature of the advice available to the practitioner is to seek structural advice that skirts the organizational defensive patterns or that assumes that these patterns do not exist.

For example, in a review of the literature on how to implement new strategic plans, I found the following advice to be most frequently recommended:

1. Define the new roles and responsibilities.
2. Find the right people to carry them out.
3. Provide these people with adequate financial support.
4. Provide them with effective information systems.
5. Reward them for taking risks and provide top management support.

The advice makes sense in that, if followed correctly, it creates sound structures and conditions. If you get the right people, then you will undoubtedly be ahead. If they get adequate financial support, effective information, and top management support, then their success is likely to be enhanced.

The problems arise when we define the new roles and responsibilities. As we see in chapter 6, this requires more than a thoughtful job description. Individuals often have many concerns, emanating from organizational defensive routines, that they try to protect against when they are defining their new roles. Unfortunately, most of these factors are undiscussable and hence are brought in by using adroit language and equally often resented by people who see their sense of responsibility threatened.

In a study of the implementation of strategies, I found cases in which top management had followed all the advice above, yet the outcome was not as effective as had been hoped. The reason was that the right person, with the right job, the right information, and top management support was frustrated by organizational defensive routines from people who apparently agreed with the new strategy and who hoped they could safely undermine it by cover-up after it was put in place, their actions drawing on organizational defensive routines.

In another study of structural advice, Bolman and Deal (1984) point out that structural advisers see problems arise from hidden structural flaws. They try to map job definitions, linkages among jobs, and organizational structure. They often find such errors as:

Overlap: Two or more individuals doing the same thing and often not realizing it. Duplicate activities waste effort and territorial disputes are common.

Gaps: Important tasks and responsibilities are not assigned correctly or fall through the cracks.

Overload: Too much work, or *Underuse,* too little work. (Bolman and Deal 1984, 51–53)

The structural solutions to these problems are to reduce overlap, to fill in gaps, and to reduce overload and underuse. Let us assume that these are accomplished well and the structural advice has worked.

But what if we asked this question: Why did people adhere to the overlap, live with gaps, tolerate overload, and protect underuse? To answer it, we then would have to dig into the organizational defensive pattern in the organization. Unless this digging is done, these problems can arise at other times or in different locations within the organization. The solution does not persist or sustain itself.

Keeping the distinction between structural and behavioral change alive may actually be an example of fancy footwork on the parts of line and of the human resources professionals. The former do not have to face their casual responsibility for the ODP. The latter could focus on providing many courses that teach new ideas and concepts (all of which could be helpful in providing understanding) but do not deal with the problems of skilled incompetence, organizational defensive routines, and fancy footwork. In the long run, as we see in chapter 6, not dealing with these problems could lessen the credibility of the new managerial theories of involvement and participation.

Management Consulting[5]

Another important source of advice and help for the practitioner is management consultants. During the past two decades, management consultants have invited me to help them with their problems in communicating information that was embarrassing or threatening to the clients. In most cases, the problem was not so much confronting a client's incompetence. Many consultants felt obliged to tell the truth to the client, even if the truth hurt.

The question was how to deal with the clients' hostile reactions when informed of their responsibilities for causing the problems. Or, how to deal with a client system in which the people in power felt that their immediate reports were not effective, and the immediate reports felt the opposite. Or, how to deal with a client who might be open to criticism on technical issues, but not on interpersonal issues. And how to do all this without losing the client.

In all the episodes I observed, the consultants used bypass strategies. In the few cases in which the consultants were more forthright, they acted consistently with Model I. This action made it easier for the clients to feel attacked and to react in a righteous manner, thereby dismissing the consultants' valid diagnoses.

Case A: A Professional Bypassing Defensive Routine

A strategy professional, extremely strong in formal, quantitative analysis as well as predisposed to engage in individual-organizational defensive routines, was faced with the following dilemma. The top executives of a large corporation were seeking a new strategy. More important, they were asking him to teach the divisional vice-presidents how to produce and implement a more effective strategy. However, the corporate officers were part of the problem and were unaware of this fact.

During a discussion with the top management, the strategy professional pointed out that a focus on the corporate strategic planning process inevitably leads to issues of organizational structure, control and reward mechanisms, communication patterns, and individual skills and behavior on the part of the senior executives at corporate and at the divisions. The consultant ordered these issues inversely in terms of importance but in the order in which he believed they would be heard. He thought the top management would have little difficulty in discussing their behavior. He

5. This section draws heavily on my book *Strategy, Change, and Defensive Routines*. 1985. New York: Ballinger.

also believed that this was the order of discussion with which he would do best. The reason he would have difficulty discussing top management skill and behavior was not that he did not have adequate data, or that he was not confident of his analysis, or that he doubted he could present his case clearly. He believed he would have difficulty because if he presented the data and analysis forthrightly, he would threaten the clients. He, in turn, was not confident about how he would deal with clients if they felt threatened. If he could not deal with these feelings effectively, then the clients could legitimately become upset.

I pause to point out two features of his decision. First, it is possible for professionals who are highly competent in formal, quantitative analysis also to be aware of critical defensive routines at the highest level. Second, and more important, if one reads the literature that cautions against too much emphasis on the measurable and suggests a greater emphasis on open, candid discussions among the top, one will find much discussion of the problem this individual faced—namely, that the behavior of the top is harming the planning process. Management consultants, however, report that this is one of the most frequent problems they face.

To return to the case, the consultant designed a presentation-discussion session. His two major objectives were to:

1. Identify top management's major reservations about the lack of effectiveness of the present planning process. These reservations included the facts that plans are overoptimistic compared to performance, that some new ventures have been less successful than expected, and that divisions present incomplete information for top management to use to make decisions.
2. Identify the divisions' major concerns. These concerns included the facts that corporate does not have a strategy, that the roles and expectations of the divisions are unclear, and that corporate emphasizes budgets more than strategy.

The consultant began by describing, in the form of a minilecture, the important features of effective strategic management in any corporation, with illustrations of weaknesses on the part of the client corporation. The material used to illustrate points (1) and (2) preceding required two slides. The material in the following discussion required sixteen slides. The point is that the emphasis placed on the discussion by the new material could make it possible for the clients to distance themselves from discussing points (1) and (2) as well as the defensive routines implied in these presentations.

The consultant also pointed out several weaknesses of the compensation scheme—for example, good/bad performance was not defined, feedback on performance was either inadequate or nonexistent, and bonuses were unrelated to performance. He then noted that such a compensation scheme implied that corporate believed that divisional management did not know what the goals of their business were, and that strategic and budgeting objectives were not reinforced. Division's reaction, in turn, was to be noncontroversial, not to rock the boat, and to maintain the status quo. The consultant concluded that the corporation must move toward a management compensation system that rewarded the attainment of previously agreed-on goals.

Next, the consultant focused on why the divisions tried to avoid controversial subjects. He suggested several possibilities, including that meetings might be too large for top management to ask tough questions, that limited time for preparation results in reactive styles, that meetings are polite with little challenge, that follow-up is limited, and that operating issues are often confused with strategic issues. The consultant ended this segment of the slide presentation by asking, "Are divisions not aware of this or is it that they believe the top expects 'onward and upward approach' and/or they fear reprisals for unfavorable forecasts?"

As we examine this material, we see that the consultant presented many important issues that are related to the organizational defensive routines. He did not, however, create the opportunity for the top to discuss these issues. Instead of stopping and encouraging discussion on these issues, he moved ahead to a section on suggestions for action steps.

The action steps included:

1. Reallocating top management between budget reviews and strategy.
2. Requiring each business to articulate its strategy for the next five years.
3. Specifying that these documents be formally accepted or rejected by the top.
4. Holding short annual strategy review meetings.
5. Implementing a compensation scheme and specifying the features.
6. Making sure the executive committee is better prepared to discuss strategy alternatives.

These six steps imply more corporate staff work—specifically, posing questions before meetings, following up after meetings, and holding smaller meetings.

Note what has happened. The consultant raised questions about defensive routines. He avoided giving all the data that he had, lest those data upset the clients. He did not encourage discussion of the questions as he was raising them. When he arrived at his suggestions, he focused on structural and administrative processes, as did most of the authors in the literature cited previously. The advice, such as posing tougher questions ahead of time or holding smaller meetings, can be implemented in such a way that the defensive routines do not get addressed.

The consultant's ambivalence is evident by the fact that he identifies the defensive routines and then bypasses them when recommending actions. Also, he never discusses the skills and actions of the top officers (corporate and divisional) that are causing the defensive routines he identified.

The consultant recalled that he went into the meeting with trepidation. He wanted to focus on difficult issues that strategy consultants are not normally expected to deal with. Being concerned about the possible negative reaction, he used the easing-in approach. The easing-in approach also led him to downplay the defensive routines at the top and to act as if he were not downplaying them. Part of downplaying them was not to present as rigorous and complete a map of the defensive routines and their consequences as was available.

The consultant's approach made it less likely not only that the clients would bypass important defenses but also that he could help the clients use some of the errors to begin to learn how to learn. For example:

The Executives Learned	*They Should Also Have Learned to Answer These Questions*
They were too soft.	What individual and organizational factors lead them to reason and act in soft ways?
They should hold smaller more frequent meetings.	What prevented them from and reaching this conclusion by themselves?
They should develop a more sophisticated planning system.	How aware were they of the gaps and errors in the planning process? What prevented them from beginning to close their gaps and correct the errors?
Divisional executives saluted corporate.	What factor leads division executives to believe that saluting is necessary? How do they hide their belief?
Strategies are often overoptimistic.	What factors lead planners to design strategies that are overoptimistic? If they know they are overoptimistic, how do they hide it? If they do not, then what does it say about their competence?

Answering the questions on the right-hand side accomplishes several important types of learning. First, the organization identifies the causal factors that inhibited the original learning as well as the factors that inhibited the executives from identifying the causal factors in the first place. Second, such causal factors are usually finite in number but almost infinite in their impact on the total functioning of the organization. Hence, identifying the factors that may inhibit learning related to planning will provide rich and relevant data about the organizational defensive routines that are related to other important topics. Third, if the clients are able to deal with the factors that inhibited their learning, then they will increase the probability that they can be masters of their destiny.

To summarize, the consultant was afraid; hence, he eased in. The clients were afraid, and they, too, eased in. The consultant reinforced the clients' fears when he also eased in. The clients then shied away from discussing the undiscussable. This, in turn, proved to the consultant that he was correct in easing in. The proof could have been a self-fulfilling prophecy in a self-sealing process.

Case B: A Strategy Professional Attempting to Deal with Colleagues' Defensive Routines

Bill is the senior professional in a corporate strategy department. During the past two years, he had studied the activities of the strategy professionals in the corporation and concluded that not enough attention was being paid to building better bridges with the line executives in order to enhance commitment and implementation. Bill's diagnosis of why this happened included the following four reasons:

1. We overanalyze instead of talking with clients.
2. We go into a presentation prepared with a rigorous analysis that we believe should make us heroes to the clients.
3. Because we do not talk enough with our clients, we do not know if and where problems may exist during the presentation.
4. We rely on our confidence in our analyses and on our ability to react quickly to questions about the validity of our analyses and, if necessary, to raise the level of proof.

Bill's diagnosis contains three causal microtheories and views of what actions to take.

Causal Problems	*Suggested Remedies*
We overanalyze and talk too little with the client.	Reduce the analysis and talk more with the client.

Causal Problems	*Suggested Remedies*
We expect that a rigorous analysis will lead the clients to feel good about us.	Reduce reliance on the rigorous analysis and on the desire to be heroes.
We are blind to the gaps and difficulties with clients during the presentations.	Become aware of gaps and difficulties during the presentations.

As in the case of the literature, the diagnoses and advice are at a very high level of inference. They combine to hide the gaps that have to be filled if the advice is to be implemented. Bill is doing to his colleagues what he is complaining they are doing with the client. For example, Bill recommends that the strategy professional should interact more with the clients and depend less on highly rigorous analysis to make them heroes.

Let us start with the advice to interact more. Let us assume that Bill believes that whatever should be said should have positive effects. Let us also assume that the strategy professionals know how to implement the advice for the easy, routine problems. But what about the problems that involve organizational defensive routines? The probability is quite high that under those conditions, the strategy professionals will activate their bypass routines. This could make it more likely that they will produce more rather than fewer difficulties with the clients.

Next, let us examine the advice not to use rigorous analysis to create hero relationships. Recall, again, that no one can knowingly design errors. If the strategy professionals use rigorous analyses to become heroes, then they are either unaware of their error or they are aware of what they are doing and are willing to do so because it makes sense to them. Under what conditions would this strategy make sense? One possibility is that strategy professionals (whom we have studied) are prone to feeling vulnerable in a client relationship when the client becomes upset or is not laudatory about the analysis. This vulnerability can upset the strategy professionals so much that they lose their cool. Losing their cool, in turn, reinforces their vulnerability. One personal bypass routine to prevent this loop from occurring is to be a hero. The dilemma is that being a hero in the eyes of the client will simultaneously distance the professional from the client. It is difficult to be close and relaxed and to feel equal with heroes.

Moreover, if the strategy professionals chose this bypass routine, they must also program themselves to be unaware of what is going on. If they were aware, they would realize that striving to be a hero is a defense; hence, it is a sign of weakness and not of strength. One way to become unaware is to place a great deal of emphasis on the importance of high-quality rigorous analysis and to believe that this emphasis is in the client's best interests.

We are now back to Bill's formulation of the problem. It is not difficult to believe these ideas if the strategy professionals have spent many hours in business-school classes, where they are taught to believe in the primary formal analysis by faculty who live a world in which they get promoted by being heroes in their respective fields.

Senior professionals often begin to examine the counterproductive features of these bypass routines because as they become senior, they also become responsible for maintaining a department or for keeping a consulting firm busy. This is the reason Bill began to reexamine the practice in his department. The difficulty is that the advice is not easily implemented.

I have had the opportunity to observe a few senior professionals who were superior at formal analysis and at creating effective relationships with clients. For example, one such senior professional realized that the presentation a subordinate colleague was making, which he had approved the day before, was not going well. He interrupted the presentation and said, "May I interrupt for a minute? I'd like to repeat what (my colleague) is saying in somewhat different words. It can be boiled down to the following. The first is caught between the devil and the deep blue sea. (Explains.) One way to solve the problem is to place your bets on . . . . If you do not, the chances are . . . (that the following will occur)."

The CEO's eyes lit up and he said, "Good; that is what I thought you people were saying, but . . . if that is your view, I want to challenge it." The consultant responded, "What are your doubts?" Note that in helping the client understand his view, the consultant also made himself more vulnerable. His willingness to be vulnerable and to deal with the confrontation that followed led the CEO to call him "my kind of consultant."

Let's go back to Bill as he was discussing his analysis with his colleagues. Most of them reacted positively. "It is a sound study," "Good ideas," were typical comments. Then, one colleague said, in effect, that they were aware of such problems and wondered if Bill understood this. Bill responded, "Of course, there is probably little that is new in this memo. I just thought it might be of value to draw the problem to our attention." They responded, "Of course."

Does that sound familiar? It is the same response that the previous consultant received from his clients when he tried to communicate some doubts he had about their effectiveness. Bill's response was also the same in that he withdrew his doubts lest he alienate himself from his colleagues. He could have asked, for example, for illustrations of how they dealt with the problem. Or he could have asked, "How could the analysis be correct and they understand it, but the problem continues?" Bill's automatic response was to bypass. His colleagues' responses were the same. The clients in the previous case were the same. All probably left their respective contexts feeling good. However, these are the very bypass routines that cause the problems in the first place.

Advice through Organizational Surveys

Another important way top management often uses to understand the human side of their enterprise is to conduct an organizational diagnosis. This diagnosis takes the form of a survey, especially in large organizations. Most of these surveys, when implemented correctly, bypass the organizational defensive patterns and thereby drive them underground in the short run and reinforce them in the long run.

The first reason for saying they bypass the organizational defensive patterns is that the rigorous methodology used to design such surveys collects information about espoused theories (beliefs, attitudes, judgments). This information provides little data from which to infer the theory-in-use.

Let us look at the questions often asked in a survey about leadership. Respondents are asked to check off (on some sort of scale, such as 1 to 5 or 1 to 7) how "considerate," "task oriented," "caring," "respectful," "strong," and so on a given superior is. The respondent thinks about his superior's actions. He may ask himself how caring or supportive is my superior. He will use a Model I meaning of caring because, as we have pointed out, most individuals hold a Model I theory-in-use.

But, as we have seen, such concepts of caring may work as long as there are no difficult problems. Model I concepts of caring, such as easing in, are a recipe for trouble if the other people involved differ seriously. But, as we have also seen, the other people do not express their differences openly because they, too, believe that caring means easing in and not upsetting others. Thus, a superior who is scored high on caring may ease in. A superior who is scored low on caring may be more forthright, but he may confront in a counterproductive mode. Both superiors are counterproductive but for different reasons.

The designers of the surveys may respond that such possibilities are rare. These possibilities can be dealt with by having a large enough sample. I am suggesting they represent the rule rather than the rare case.

Another fundamental problem is that the knowledge gained from these surveys on such topics as leadership, disempowerment, initiative, and risk taking is difficult to use in order to take action.

The creators of the surveys are aware of this problem. One way they bridge the gap between knowledge and action is to create what are often called *action groups*. These groups are given the statistical results and asked to define what the results mean for the departments they represent. They are also asked to suggest solutions. The suggestions are forwarded to a corporate action group that makes the final recommendation.

These action groups are relatively effective when the problems they are dealing with are straightforward. For example, if people reported that they were underpaid, a study could be conducted to compare their salaries with those for comparable work in the same geographic area. The same procedure would be followed for complaints about retirements benefits, paid vacation, and so on.

The more we deal with problems that are caused by the organizational defensive pattern, however, the more that very pattern takes hold during the discussions in the action groups intended to make sense of the data. I have frequently observed conversations full of mixed messages, defensive reasoning, unawareness, and inconsistencies in which disagreement and polarization abound.

One way the designers of these surveys deal with such threats is to create rules that attempt to reduce the polarization. Any idea can be sent upward if one person in the action group insists. The result of this procedure is that ideas do get sent up to the final committee, the corporate action group. This committee, however, often finds itself inundated with recommendations that appear to its members to be unclear, vague, inconsistent and, at times, unusable because to use them would make someone feel embarrassed or threatened. The committee members, in turn, develop action recommendations that are vague and general and that bypass and cover up possible causes of embarrassment or threat.

For example, a survey showed that many respondents at all levels misunderstood the role of the personnel division in a large corporation. The final action committee recommended:

- Better communication by personnel of the division's role.
- A more clear and complete mission statement.
- Defining and teaching new skills and competences required by personnel administrators.

The logic is that the personnel division's role is misunderstood by the rest of the organization. Therefore, clear up the misunderstanding with new mission statements and new communication effort. Also, retrain people who need further skill training.

I analyzed some of the tape-recorded discussions in the action groups that led to this diagnosis. Actually, many line people did not misunderstand personnel's role. They understood it and disagreed with it *or* they questioned the competence of personnel people to implement their mission. However, to say this candidly was seen as a recipe for causing defensiveness; hence, the softer phrasing was used in order for the message to be heard.

But, as we see, the personnel division representatives took the message seriously and sent to its top people recommendations that dealt with the problem as described. The logic embedded in this action was:

If there is a hole in the minds of other people about the role of Personnel	then	Fill the hole with valid and clear information about the role.
If other people hold views about Personnel performance that are negative	then	Provide them the correct information that should (if they are reasonable people) lead them to change their negative evaluations.

Imagine the employees and managers who are eventually shown a new mission statement or exposed to training sessions about the role of personnel and who believe that these are not the crucial problems. They, understandably, throw up their hands. Their reactions are to dismiss the new mission statement as too abstract and to sit through the communication program as patiently as they can. Their patience may be due to the realization that they helped create these seminars by sending up the smoothed over diagnosis about personnel in the first place.

Or, consider the example in which several long discussions were held about the ineffectiveness of the leadership at the top. The problem was how to communicate the negative findings to the top. After several meetings with no agreement, a subgroup was asked to write a version of their findings. They massaged and crafted a version that pleased most.

The negative views were smoothed over, and, of course, the smoothing over was covered up. For example:

> "It's been rewarding to find Senior Management so responsive and ready to deal with the issues we brought to them."
>
> "Both the survey data and the issue statements expressed employees' concerns with leadership at all levels of the company. Specific issues centered around the credibility of management, overall company management, and accountability."

The committee members who delivered the message reported that they were "more specific" when they met with the top. They made specific recommendations that the top delegate authority, give in-house experts a voice in decision making, establish lines of responsibility and accountability, and update leadership behavior and style to match current trends.

Imagine if you were the top receiving such messages. What is concrete about them? Would you not feel, as they did, that there was not much new in the recommendations? Would you also not feel, as did those at the top, that the people below who made these recommendations do not understand what is really going on?

Conclusion

In order for advice to be implementable or enactable, it must:

- *Contain a causal theory, such as, if you act in such-and-such manner, the following will happen.*
- *Illustrate the "such-and-such" manner at two levels. First, the advice should contain the action strategies (e.g., advocate your position in a way that encourages inquiry). Second, it should be accompanied with actual statements that illustrate what you would have to say and do.*
- *Include the values that should be governing the action strategies. For example, if you encourage inquiry in order to be consistent with Model I values (win, be in unilateral control, etc.) you will be seen as lawyering—as asking questions in order to nail someone. (In chapter 6 we describe a different theory-in-use in which the same action strategies are used in order to generate valid information, informed choice, and internal commitment. This, as we see, requires a different type of conversation.*

The advice that we have reviewed did not contain all three of these characteristics. The causal theories were rarely explicit. The action strategies were frequently stated, but they were not illustrated by what individuals should say and do to enact them. It was difficult, therefore, to figure out how to implement them. It was also difficult to decide what values were being used. This gap is critical, because if you advise people to abhor defensive routines, and if you then give advice that bypasses and covers up the defensive routines, then it is unlikely that your advice will be seen as credible.

If the receivers sense that you are unaware of the discrepancy, they, too (in line with Model I), cover up their reactions and act quite positively. They will try to save your face and their own and will act as if they are not doing so.

These characteristics of advice exist in the field of consulting on managing the human side of the enterprise, especially when embarrassment and threat exist. Moreover, in my experience of senior level executive programs at universities and within large corporations, the same goes on. In short, the advice available for changing skilled incompetence, organizational defensive

Rung		
4	The theories we use to create the meanings on rung 3	
3	Meanings imposed by us	
2	Culturally understood meanings	
1	Relatively directly observable data, such as conversations	

Figure 5.1 ***Ladder of Inference***

routines, fancy footwork, and malaise is either inadequate or implemented in ways that reinforce these factors.

Much of the advice about how to deal with organizational defenses and fancy footwork either ignores the realities of changing them or actually exacerbates the problem.

One reason is that the reasoning the authors use to craft the advice is caught up in a dilemma related to how the human mind works. Picture a ladder of inference (see Figure 5.1). On the first rung of the ladder are the relatively directly observable data, such as the actual conversations and nonverbal cues that are used.

The second rung represents the culturally understood meanings that individuals with different views or different axes to grind would agree were communicated during the conversation. For example, a superior or subordinate might agree that the former told the latter that his performance was unacceptable.

The third rung of the ladder represents the meanings that individuals impose on the second-rung meanings. For example, the superior might say that he was honest and forthright. The subordinate might call the same actions blunt and insensitive.

The fourth rung represents the theories of action individuals use to craft their conversations and to understand the actions of other people.

This ladder of inference shows, for example, that the evaluations or judg-

ments people make automatically are not concrete or obvious. They are abstract and highly inferential. Individuals treat them as if they were concrete because they produce them so automatically that they do not even think that their judgments are highly inferential. The fallacy of misplaced concreteness, identified years ago by the philosopher Sir Alfred North Whitehead, is a natural by-product of this skill.

The ladder of inference helps us explain the defensive reasoning embedded in the advice described in this chapter. First, this advice rarely included the actual conversation (not to mention the nonverbal cues). The reader has no idea of the actual conversation that was crafted. The advice was primarily at the second or third rung of the ladder—for example, "be caring," "show concern," or "encourage participation." What we find is that when individuals hear such advice or give it to themselves, they have in mind that it will produce positive consequences. To use our language, they think of consequences that are consistent with Model II theory-in-use and with social virtues.

When they act, however, almost all act consistently with Model I. As we have seen, caring in the Model I manner eventually leads to noncaring consequences. The actors, who are unaware of what they are producing, explain the counterproductive consequences by blaming the other people.

We can predict a generic pattern of misunderstanding that goes something like this:

- *The giver of the advice espouses actions that are consistent with Model II.*
- *The receivers understand the advice with Model II in mind.*
- *When the receivers try to act out the advice, however, they have to use their theory-in-use, which in most cases means Model I, and therefore they get into trouble.*
- *The receivers may then hold the adviser responsible for giving poor advice or may blame the others for becoming defensive.*

There should be a warning label on advice on how to deal with difficult human problems. The label should say:

> *It is unlikely that you will be able to produce this advice when you are dealing with issues that contain components of embarrassment or threat. You are likely to be unaware of this fact while you are implementing this advice. Or, if you are aware, you will tend to blame factors other than yourself.*

The time has arrived to present a different theory-in-use and different social virtues that, if implemented correctly and consistently, should lead to reduction of the organizational defensive pattern.

References

Argyris, Chris. 1986. *Strategy, Change, and Defensive Routines*. Boston: Ballinger.

Bolman, Lee, and Terrence Deal. 1984. *Modern Approaches to Understanding and Managing Organizations*. San Francisco: Jossey-Bass.

Bruce, James S. 1986. *The Intuitive Pragmatists: Conversations with Chief Executive Officers*. Greensboro, NC: Center for Creative Leadership.

Burns, James MacGregor. 1978. *Leadership*. New York: Harper & Row.

Drucker, Peter F. 1985. *New Management*, vol. 3: "Drucker on Drucker," 7–9.

———. 1966. *The Effective Executive*. New York: Harper & Row.

———. 1973. *Management*. New York: Harper & Row.

Horton, Thomas R. 1986. *What Works for Me*. New York: Random House Business Division. Reprinted by permission of the author.

Kappel, Frederick R. 1964. *Validity in Business Enterprise*. New York: McKinsey Foundation for Management Research, Graduate School of Business, Columbia University.

Mills, D. Quinn. 1985. *The New Competitors: A Report on American Managers*. New York: John Wiley & Sons.

Chapter Six

Reducing the Organizational Defense Pattern

▸ During a retreat with the top management of a 7-billion-dollar decentralized organization, the CEO learned that corporate–division relationships were not as good as he had thought. The top management identified four problems.

1. The philosophy and meaning of decentralization were not clear; corporate often violated divisional space.
2. Corporate staff felt that they lacked adequate authority to deal with the line.
3. Overlapping responsibilities existed among corporate staff roles.
4. Corporate staff felt that they did not have adequate contact with the CEO.

The CEO charged a task force of line and corporate staff with (1) redefining the roles in order to eliminate confusion, (2) defining adequate authority to deal with line, and (3) defining appropriate contacts for line and staff with the CEO. The task force finished its work ahead of time. The top group met and approved it with minor alterations. We have a happy ending.

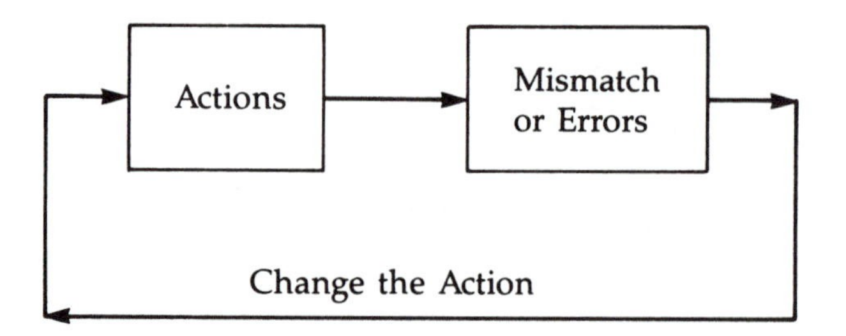

Figure 6.1 ***Single-Loop Learning***

It depends. Let us review the events. The task force reflected on the errors of existing actions and recommended how to correct them.

Figure 6.1 illustrates single-loop learning. A thermostat is a single-loop learner. It detects when the air around it is too hot or too cold and corrects the situation by turning the heat on or off. The task force detected the incorrect actions and corrected them.

Single-loop learning solves the presenting problems. It does not solve the more basic problem of *why* these problems existed in the first place. For example, the corporate staff and divisional officers (1) adhered to policies that they described as inadequate, (2) implemented staff roles that they said produced confusion, and (3) maintained inadequate authority among the relationship between policies and staff roles. These three actions, by their own diagnosis, were errors. The question is, Why did the top officers adhere to, implement, and maintain these errors for several years?

I asked the top management group that question. After some bewilderment and pausing, the answers began to surface. The answers included (1) divisional management's fear that corporate staff was making significant inroads on their authority, (2) corporate staff's fear that they did not wish to use their expertise because it would mean that divisional management were admitting weakness, and (3) both corporate staff and divisional presidents' playing politics to get the CEO's attention.

These answers radically altered the nature of the problem. We have moved from causes that have little to do with features of the organizational defensive pattern to causes that are intimately connected with the pattern. We moved into this frame because someone refused to take for granted what was being taken for granted.

> Individuals were adhering to errors. They were taking for granted the errors as well as adhering to the errors.
>
> Errors produced under these conditions are designed errors. They are not due to ignorance.

> The next step was to ask the individuals what led them to adhere to, maintain, and proliferate actions that they had diagnosed as errors.

This step led to a discussion that illustrated many organizational defensive routines and fancy footwork. For example, divisional line management saw the corporate financial officer (CFO) as undermining their authority by reporting to the CEO what he learned during visits at the divisions. "Why shouldn't he tell me what he discovers?" asked the CEO. "Because we should tell you first," they replied. "Fine. Why not tell him that?" asked the CEO. "Because those types of issues are never discussed." "I'll add another one that is probably not discussed. Namely, that you divisional presidents must think either that I ask for or condone the CFO and other corporate staff to take on the role of organizational Gestapo. I'd like to discuss that issue." The discussion brought out more organizational defensive routines and fancy footwork coupled with strategies corporate staff aand divisional line officers use to distance themselves from these problems and to cover up the distances.

I then asked a divisional president what he would say to the CFO if he were to speak candidly to him. The divisional president thought for a moment and said, "Well, I guess that I would tell him that I was fed up . . . no. Hold it, I was concerned about the fact that he was undermining my relationship with the CEO."

This response illustrated skilled unawareness and incompetence. If the divisional president were to tell the CFO that he was fed up with the CFO's undermining behavior, the CFO might understandably feel prejudged and misjudged. He might feel that the divisional president's response had no basis in fact. I then asked other people how they would react. All of them said they would file their reactions away as something to discuss with the divisional president at another time. They would not discuss such things now because the divisional president was obviously upset, and they too were likely to be upset.

Let's review the responses. The divisional president's responses indicated what he had kept hidden and covered up, namely, that he was fed up about the CFO's behavior. But his ideas and feelings were untested attributions and evaluations. They are reminiscent of the left-hand columns of the officers in chapter 2. Note also that the recipients of his responses also bypassed what they considered hostile comments and covered up that they were doing so. Again, they acted like the senior executives did in chapter 2. Asking executives with a Model I theory-in-use to become candid can be a recipe for trouble because their actions are governed by the values of win, don't lose.

These errors cannot be corrected simply by designing new actions. To correct these actions, we must first alter the governing values. This

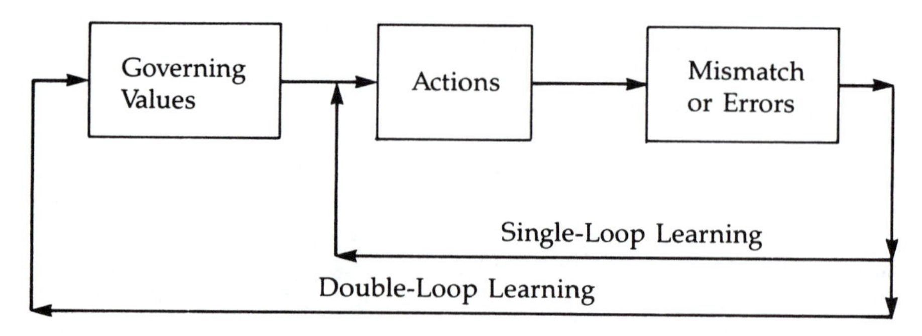

Figure 6.2 ***Double-Loop Learning***

means we have to learn a new theory-in-use. This is double-loop learning (see Figure 6.2).

The top management group in this story had two different problems to solve. The first problem was to rewrite the rules and policies of corporate-staff relationships. They accomplished this to their satisfaction. As far as they were concerned there was a happy ending because they had solved the problems they had identified.

The second problem was to solve the problem that the executives had adhered to and for which they had maintained the errors for several years. What organizational defensive routine, fancy footwork, and malaise made these actions possible?

It is more important to solve these problems because they created the problems of ineffective roles and policies; they permitted these problems to exist; and they caused the bypassing and cover-up. As long as these defensive factors exist, it will be difficult for the organization to be a double-loop learner. At best, it will solve the single-loop problems, only to find several months or years later they have surfaced in a new way.

The Nature of the New Advice

In short, the advice is: Develop the players' capacity to produce double-loop learning. Teach them a new theory-in-use; call it Model II:

- Develop a culture that rewards Model II actions. It relegates Model I actions to the routine, easy problems that do not require long-term monitoring for effective implementation.
- Put in place rewards that encourage individuals to learn how to decrease their skilled incompetence and their contributions to the organizational defensive routines, fancy footwork, and malaise.

How to Get from Here to There

The first step in empowering an organization with the capacity to learn, especially around problems that are embarrassing and threatening, is to map out how the organization presently deals with such problems. For example, we ask the players to identify a vexing problem that they wish they could solve but have been unable to solve and cannot conceive of a solution to because so many defenses are involved.

One candidate is pay for performance. It has always been a policy for management to pay for performance. Yet, this has rarely been done. Currently, a spate of new programs exists to get the job done. And, if I may be permitted a prediction, most of the better programs will lead to a little progress largely because of the thoughtful technical design features developed by compensation experts. The prediction is that this progress will be reversed in a few years. The reason is that most pay-for-performance programs bypass the organizational defensive routines, fancy footwork, and malaise that cause them in the first place. These programs do not help each player, especially those at the top, to become aware of how each contributes to the defenses that he or she decries.

This leads to the second step in empowering an organization with the capacity to learn. Once the organizational map is developed, the next step is to help the individual players diagnose the extent to which each contributes to creating and maintaining the map. To take this step, we have the players develop a map of their personal theories-in-use when dealing with pay-for-performance problems that are embarrassing or threatening. This map should be constructed in a way that permits each player an opportunity to generate insights into his or her skilled incompetence. The map need not be limited to pay-for-performance problems. It could illuminate how the players activate other organizational defensive factors.

The third step is to reeducate the players to take Model II from an espoused theory to a theory-in-use. The good news is that for most individuals the primary ingredient in this step is practice, especially as they are dealing with everyday organizational problems.

Reeducation, however, is difficult to the extent the individuals are embarrassed and threatened about learning a new theory-in-use. As long as they see the opportunity to learn as a positive one, the prognosis is quite good. It will take as much time to learn Model II as it takes to play a middling game of tennis. So far, the majority of the executives with whom we have worked have had the capacity to learn Model II without too much difficulty.

The fourth step is to repeat the learning experience to solve new problems as they arise. In other words, as individuals learn new theory-in-use they begin to apply it to double-loop problems as the problems arise.

Developing an Action Map around Pay for Performance

Let us look at an example of an action map around the problem of pay for performance. At the outset, the management framed the problems as follows. Too many people are receiving high ratings; managers are not being tough enough in penalizing the poor performers.

The solution was to request the compensation experts to develop a new system that would more effectively coerce a spread in the ratings and would require managers to be tougher. As a single-loop solution, this approach makes sense. The compensation officials did, in fact, develop some new technical features that would induce a greater spread of rankings.

Because the senior compensation officials had gone through the learning experiences described above, they saw that the innovative technical solutions were going to be seriously impaired and limited by the organizational defensive routines, fancy footwork, and malaise. They asked Robert Putnam and Dolores Thomas to develop an action map in order to show why this was so.

In order to set the context for the map, let us begin with the compensation policy in operation in 1971. The policy was based on the assigned content of the job and how well it was performed. The two values underlying the program were fairness (people doing the same work should be paid the same) and growth (people should be able to grow to their maximum potential). The organization at that time was growing, had high profitability, and had many promotion opportunities.

By 1987, although the same policy and the same values were in place, the conditions had changed in three ways. First, the economic growth had slowed down, and hence the promotion opportunities had diminished. Second, technological changes had been instituted by which it was possible to produce the same with less employee work. Third, organizational innovations such as job redesign had been introduced to give the employees more opportunities for involvement and hence greater productivity.

In theory, an organization that is as enlightened and thoughtful as this one should be able to manage the transition from the early to the present conditions. But several trends had been developing since 1971 that made implementing the new compensation scheme more difficult.

- Employees received high performance ratings even though their performance was only good or average. The high performance ratings became expected and normal. As a result, there was little differentiation on the basis of performance. Most individuals progressed to the top of the scale largely through seniority. Few additional rewards were therefore available for exceptional performers.
- The employees' attention shifted from performance to preserving their jobs and accumulating overtime. Few sought to take on new tasks because there were no rewards for such actions. Yet the company's orientations were toward reducing overtime and enlarging jobs.

These trends led to three organizational dilemmas:

- Pressure was exerted on managers and supervisors to give employees "good" to "high" reviews in order not to upset them. But as a majority of employees reached the "exceptional" level at the top of the scale, pressure was exerted not to give further increases.
- As high performers saw that mediocre performers received the same rewards, they felt treated unjustly and also sensed that their co-workers might see them as a threat to overtime. But if the high performers backed off, they would be violating their own standard of responsibility.
- As supervisors saw slippage among the employees at the top of the scale, their sense of stewardship implied that those employees should receive lower ratings. But taking pay away was not an accepted norm; indeed, it could create a grievance.

The trends and their consequences violated the rules and values of pay for performance. The economic downturn exacerbated their impact. In other words, supervisors, in the high economic slack days, dealt with the embarrassing and potentially threatening issues of giving the average to low performers commensurate ratings by bypassing the problems and covering up the bypass. The economic downturn made the cover-ups no longer acceptable. By that time, however, the organizational norms were in place that made adhering to the original values unjust and uncaring.

How did a pay for performance based on justice and caring become a program for injustice and uncaring? The basis for injustice was built during the good economic times; here, I refer to the generic defensive rules that managers, at all levels, used to deal with the potential embarrassment and threat of giving mediocre to low performers mediocre to poor or no advances in pay.

Putnam and Thomas (1988) described the generic rules:

Don't upset people.

Keep things calm.

Deal with inequities privately.

This pattern of rules is a recipe for continuing the bypass and the cover-up. These consequences, in turn, are consistent with Model I notions of caring and support (don't upset people, keep everyone happy, etc.). Changing the pay-for-performance program thus would become a threat to the organizational defensive routines that had become taken for granted.

The supervisors and managers who, in the 1980s, wished to return to the original values in the compensation scheme of justice and concern would find themselves in a dilemma: If they tried to implement the new policy, they could be seen as unjust and uncaring. If they did not confront the mediocre performance, they would be covering up the problem and also covering up their cover-up. In effect this would be acting irresponsibly.

Although the top management acknowledged that the bypass activities existed and that these bypass activities were protected by organizational defensive routines, they hoped to overcome these problems by instituting smarter pay-for-performance systems. For example, a new compensation system was designed that required the supervisors to become tougher, to document their ratings more clearly, and through various forms of forced distribution to reduce the number of individuals given high ratings. The results were successful changes of the pay distribution and of the shape of the curve. Presumably, people were receiving more honest ratings.

These actions, however, had little or no impact on the quality of performance review discussions or on performance itself. For example, the CEO asked a group of supervisors and managers, "What do you tell someone when you give less than the structural pay increase?" The reply was, "We tell them that their pay is already in line with their performance." He then asked a group of employees, "What does your boss tell you when you get less than the structural pay increase?" They replied, "They tell us the money isn't in the budget."

The bypass activities continued regardless of the compensation program because the supervisors and managers were skilled at the bypass and cover-up and because the organizational defensive routines and fancy footwork supported these actions.

Putnam and Thomas told the top management that they had at least two options. The first was to act within the existing organizational defensive routines. If they did so, then they should make it explicit that they recognized that such a plan ran into the limits imposed by these organizational defensive routines and fancy footwork.

The reason for being candid was not to create false expectations about how much would be changed by the new plan. Otherwise, Putnam and Thomas predicted, a couple of years from now this plan could be used as evidence for skepticism that the next new plan would not really make a difference.

The second option that they recommended was to engage the features of the organizational defensive patterns that discouraged honest pay for performance. They suggested that the program should begin with the top. It was not likely that supervisors or employees were going to believe that the organizational defensive patterns should be dismantled unless they saw the top management engaged in such dismantling. Moreover, it was unlikely that they would feel safe to take the risks involved unless the top management had encouraged them to do so, not simply by words but by their own deeds.

Top management appeared to understand the logic of this second option. The CEO and several senior officers were in favor of the second thrust. Their concerns were about whether the human resources professionals could design and implement a reeducational and change program.

Other top executives felt that the second alternative would require too much time. They agreed that the dilemmas had taken several decades to develop. They had difficulty, however, in accepting a three- to five-year time in which to alter the actions, norms, and culture that had caused the dilemmas; they wanted a quicker fix. The same individuals also argued that the organizational defensive routines and fancy footwork could not be changed because they were based on "human nature, and you can't change that."

When combined, these two arguments produced self-sealing logic and self-fulfilling processes. If human nature could not be changed, and if any program had to bring about change quickly, then whatever program was designed would not change the behavioral patterns. This particular program might have the appearance of success. The truth, however, would be covered up and, of course, the cover-up also would be covered up.

The story can be depicted as a map with four features (see Figure 6.3). The first features are the *governing conditions* that existed when the new performance scheme was designed. The second are the *action strategies* that the managers, at all levels, were using—namely, smoothing or cover-up. Putnam and Thomas showed in detail the different smoothing or engaging strategies used at different levels. The third features are the

GOVERNING CONDITIONS	ACTION STRATEGIES	FIRST-ORDER CONSEQUENCES	SECOND-ORDER CONSEQUENCES	THIRD-ORDER CONSEQUENCES
Low economic growth	Smoothing cover-up	Increase wage bill		Influence at local level not credible
No bonuses		Natural progression to top of scale	Grievance procedures	Mistrust
Views on mediocre to poor performance differ		Appearance of calm		Polarization
	Engaging		Review board	
Company norms of: Caring • treat all alike • do not upset Others • bypass and cover-up agreements		Resentment by good performers or poor performers		Less coaching
		Protection of mediocre performance		Acceptance of mediocre performance

Figure 6.3 ***Organizational Action Map: Pay and Performance***

Source: Robert Putnam and Dolores Thomas (1988).

consequences of the action strategies. These consequences are placed in sequential order. The map in Figure 6.3 shows three sets of consequences. The fourth features of the map are the *feedback processes that reinforce* each other to make the system self-perpetuating and antilearning.

Figure 6.3 shows how the new pay-for-performance scheme will be undermined. The counterproductive features of the map cannot be corrected unless the smoothing over strategies are altered and the mistrust, polarization, acceptance of mediocrity and other factors are dealt with, which then should lead to a reexamination of the Review Board and grievance procedures.

Reducing the smoothing over requires helping the managers become aware of their theory-in-use and skilled incompetence and then helping them alter it. Reducing the mistrust, polarization, and acceptance of mediocrity requires altering the organizational defensive routines and fancy footwork that produce these factors. The latter cannot be altered effectively unless the theories-in-use are first altered. How can this be done? The first step is to help the players develop an action map of how they contribute to the program.

Individual Action Maps

Let us look at another example to illustrate the nature of individual action maps in order to show how widely they are applicable. Everything described below can easily apply to the development of the executives' action maps around pay for performance.

Recall the case described in chapter 2. In that case, the top management group identified an important problem, namely, their inability to devise an effective business strategy. Recall also that they had several meetings that were unsuccessful because of how they communicated with each other.

The first step toward change was a two-day session away from the office. The agenda of the sessions were the cases that they wrote ahead of time, as described in chapter 2.

Cases as an Intervention Tool

What is the advantage of using the cases? The cases, crafted and written by the executives themselves, become vivid examples of skilled incompetence. They vividly illustrate the skill with which each executive tried not to upset the others and to persuade them to change their position. They also vividly illustrate the incompetence component because the results, by their own analysis, were to upset the others and to make it less likely that their own views would prevail.

The cases are also very important learning devices. It is difficult for anyone to slow down the behavior that they produce in milliseconds during a real meeting in order to reflect on it and change it. The danger is that other people will grab control of the air time available. Moreover, it is difficult for the human mind to pay attention to both interpersonal actions and to substantive issues at the same time.

Why not have an outside person act as a facilitator to make the conversation more effective? I did act as a facilitator for a while. But this is not a sound solution for several reasons.

If the facilitator is successful, it is because he or she acts as a traffic cop by rephrasing the conversation whenever it is necessary, clarifying issues, pointing out messages that may be upsetting others, and so on. This is a short-term solution. The long-term solution is for the executives themselves to learn to do these things well. In other words, a facilitator ultimately is a person who helps the group bypass its defensive routines instead of helping the group learn to engage these routines in order to get rid of them.

Why not have the group sit down and talk about the strategy issues? The answer is that they told us that they had tried this several times and it had not worked.

One reason for this lack of success may be that it is unlikely that individuals will make public, in a regular meeting, what is in their left-hand columns. Yet, as we saw, what individuals choose to censor has an important impact, because the individuals not only cover up that they are censoring something but they also strive to cover up the cover-up. The irony is that the other group members sense this but they too cover up that they sense it, and they too cover up their cover-up.

We saw that the executives found analyzing their cases to be an eye-opener. They saw how Model I actions led to dynamics that made it difficult for them to be effective as a group. The next step was to redesign their cases.

Redesigning Their Actions

In beginning to redesign their actions, the executives turned to their cases. Each executive selected an episode that he wished to redesign so it would not have negative consequences. As an aid in their redesign, the executives were given some handouts that described a different set of behaviors. The first thing the executives realized was that they would have to slow down. They could not produce a new conversation in the milliseconds to which they were accustomed. This troubled them a bit because they were impatient to learn. They kept reminding themselves that learning new skills does require that they slow down.

One technique they used was that each individual crafted by himself a new conversation to help the writer of the episode. After taking five or so minutes, they shared their conversation with the writer. In the process of discussing these designs, the writer learned much about how to redesign his own words. But the designers also learned much as they discovered the bugs in their suggestions and how they had made these bugs.

The dialogue was very constructive, cooperative, and helpful. Typical comments about it included:

> "If you want to reach me, try it the way Joe just said."
>
> "I realize that your intentions are clean, but those words push my button (for such and such reason)."
>
> "I understand what you are trying to say, but it doesn't work for me because. . . . How about trying it this way?"
>
> "I'm impressed as to how my designs have some of the old messages. This will take time."

Practice is important. Most people required as much practice as is required to play a not-so-decent game of tennis. But practice does not need to occur all at once. The practice can occur in actual business meetings in which people set aside some time to reflect on their actions and to correct them. An outside facilitator could help them examine and redesign their actions just as a tennis coach might do. But, as in the case of a good tennis coach, the facilitator should be replaced by the group itself. The facilitator might be brought in for periodic boosters or to help when the problem is of a degree of difficulty and intensity not experienced before.

There are several consequences of this type of change program. The executives began to experience each other as being more supportive and constructive. They began to see, for example, that some of their own attributions about the others' narrow focus or competitiveness were correct. However, they also began to see that the attribution that there were issues undiscussable and not influenceable was wrong. Colleagues were not as resistant or rigid as each had attributed they were. To their pleasant surprise, the executives found that there existed much more readiness for learning than they had predicted.

This is an important discovery because it means the self-censoring and the attribution about "nothing will make these strong egos change" can now be reduced. This reduction, in turn, means that individuals can begin to say relevant things that they had been withholding.

The next problem is crafting the new conversation. If the individuals' left-hand columns are full of such statements as "Like hell you are glad to see me" and "Why don't you stop being so parochial?" then stating these thoughts that way is likely to lead to further defensive actions. All of these thoughts are crafted in the Model I manner. If they are moved to the right-hand column they will not be helpful.

When executives asked, with a good deal of incredulity, "Do you *really* want me to be blunt; wouldn't that upset people?" I respond that indeed it would upset people. The new theory-in-use does not advise people to think in Model I terms; it also does not assume that somehow if you are candid it will work. It will not.

The next steps are to think about these problems and to craft the conversations according to a different theory-in-use as well as a different set of meanings to the social virtues of help, respect, strength, honesty, and integrity. What do this new theory-in-use and social virtues look like?

The New Theory-in-Use

Model II is the new theory-in-use. The governing values of Model II theory-in-use are valid information, informed choice, and responsibility to monitor how well the choice is implemented.

Human beings seek to produce as much valid information as possible about an issue or problem. They have a learning orientation.

The reason for seeking information is to make choices or decisions that are as well-informed as possible. The more valid information that is available, the more likely that the decisions made will be based on the best information available.

Finally, individuals are viewed as being responsible for their decisions. Their responsibility includes monitoring how well they design and implement their decisions in order to detect and correct errors. Self-responsibility therefore invites more learning, and we are back to the first governing value.

The action strategies are to (1) advocate your position and encourage inquiry or confirmation of it, and (2) minimize face saving. The first strategy is accomplished by being forthright in expressing your views, while at the same time providing illustrations of relatively directly observable data, such as what the person said, so that the other person can see how you arrived at your premises. The idea is stating your conclusion explicitly so that you or others can examine it.

A second action strategy is to minimize taking unilateral face-saving actions. Deciding that someone else's face should be saved is an act of mistrust of the other person's capacities. Such acts ought to be tested; otherwise we are playing God with other human beings. There may be occasions when a sound test leads us to conclude that the other person would be seriously harmed by learning the truth, and thus it would not make sense to be candid. I am not saying that we should never act to save face.

To repeat, I am not saying that to tell the truth means that people should make public exactly what they censor and hide. If what people hide are unillustrated and untested negative evaluations (she failed or messed up) or unillustrated and untested attributions (he's handing me a line or is playing a power game), then to make these evaluations and attributions public as they are would be to act consistently with Model I. Individuals using Model II reason differently. They have on the left-hand column evaluations and attributions that are illustrated and tested, even though they may not always be made public, because to do so would control the time available for conversation.

Productive Reasoning

Productive reasoning goes along with Model II. Individuals strive to make their premises and inferences explicit and clear. They develop conclusions that are publicly testable. The tests are implemented in ways that are independent of the logic used by the actor so that the reasoning used to test an idea is not self-referential. That is, the criteria for finding something to be true or false should be separate from the logic of the actor who wants to find out.

While taking action, actors reflect in order to be aware of their thoughts and feelings. They hold private conversations with themselves in order to be as clear as possible about the position they are advocating and about any evaluations or attributions they may be making.

Actors seek to check constantly for any unrecognized gaps or inconsistencies and encourage other people to do the same. They also combine taking initiative with being open with any constructive confrontation of views, evaluations, or attributions.

Our research indicates that these actions slow down the actors temporarily because individuals are not skilled at using productive reasoning for issues that contain embarrassment or threat. However, once having mastered these skills, even moderately well, equal or less time is then required to say what they wish to say. What drops significantly is the amount of time individuals or groups use to defend themselves, to use their fancy footwork, and to act as if they are not doing so. Conversation moves faster with less friction or information garbage to delay it.

Model II is not the opposite of Model I. The opposite of Model I would mean adopting such governing values as everyone should be in control and all should win; it would mean suppressing rational thoughts and instead expressing feelings. These are useful values. The problem with them is that they are not realistic when work has to get done, performance to be evaluated, and striving for excellence to be maintained. Under these conditions, there are times when not everyone can be in control or win. Moreover, it is necessary for human beings to be rational as well as emotional. Using the opposite of Model I is a recipe for immobilizing action. It could lead to requiring all relevant people to participate in decisions. In the 1970s many writers recommended such conditions in the administration of organizations, schools, or communities. We now know that these conditions can be self-limiting, especially if people are encouraged to participate while dealing with their skilled incompetence and the organizational defensive routines and fancy footwork.

Using Model II leads to a reduction of misunderstanding, error, self-fulfilling prophecies, and self-sealing processes. The threshold of what is embarrassing and threatening rises. People can be more constructively candid with each other and therefore can see less need to bypass and to cover up the bypass.

Model II Social Virtues

The new theory-in-use implies new social virtues. These virtues are described in the right-hand column below and are compared with the Model I social virtues in the left-hand column.

Model I Social Virtues	Model II Social Virtues
Help and Support	
Give approval and praise to others. Tell others what you believe will make them feel good about themselves. Reduce their feelings of hurt by telling them how much you care, and, if possible, agree with them that the others acted improperly.	Increase the others' capacity to confront their own ideas, to create a window into their own mind, and to face their unsurfaced assumptions, biases, and fears by acting in these ways toward other people.
Respect for Others	
Defer to other people and do not confront their reasoning or actions.	Attribute to other people a high capacity for self-reflection and self-examination without becoming so upset that they lose their effectiveness and their sense of self-responsibility and choice. Keep testing this attribution opening.

	Model II Social Virtues
	Strength
Advocate your position in order to win. Hold your own position in the face of advocacy. Feeling vulnerable is a sign of weakness.	Advocate your position and com it with inquiry and self-reflection. Feeling vulnerable while encouraging inquiry is a sign of strength.
	Honesty
Tell other people no lies or tell others all you think and feel.	Encourage yourself and other people to say what they know yet fear to say. Minimize what would otherwise be subject to distortion and cover-up of the distortion.
	Integrity
Stick to your principles, values, and beliefs.	Advocate your principles, values, and beliefs in a way that invites inquiry into them and encourages other people to do the same.

Conditions of the Change Processes That Are Assuring

Model II is not a new or alien concept to most individuals. Governing values such as producing valid information, informed choice, and personal responsibility are espoused by most thoughtful practitioners.

Happiness, satisfaction, and feeling good, however, are not governing values. Individuals can learn to be satisfied and to feel good about the protection that organizational defensive routines, fancy footwork, and malaise can give to mediocre performance. Individuals who act in ways that overprotect themselves or others will not feel particularly happy about moving from here to there.

- The participants choose whether they wish to learn as well as how fast they will do so. They can slow down, speed up, or stop the learning processes as they choose.
- The change process begins with diagnoses of problems that the participants define as important. They write cases that they judge to illustrate the nontrivial problems they wish to overcome. We sit in and observe meetings that deal with complex issues that they create. The organizational action maps that we develop become a basis for change only after the participants say that these maps are valid.
- Every step of the way is designed as a mini-experiment. The experiment, designed by the participants, has clear guideposts

to tell them how well they are doing and has clear outcomes to judge results.

- Another control is that all the problem-solving processes designed to solve a particular problem should be usable to solve other problems. In other words, the road built from here to there should be usable for many journeys in many years to come. Therefore, they can test whether what they are learning is limited or can be generalized.
- There is no arbitrary deadline by which the learning should be finished. Indeed, becoming a learning organization usually is so intrinsically satisfying to the participants that they keep extending the learning. Although the idea of learning becomes unlimited, the intention is to use the learning to solve a particular problem. Inquiry for its own sake is not preferred. Inquiry is combined with taking action. This combination is important not only because it provides criteria to evaluate the success or failure by what is actually going on in the organization. Equally important is that individuals often diagnose problems differently if they know that they must produce an outcome than if the outcome itself is limited to being insightful.

To put it succinctly, the criterion that learning occurs is not simply have the individuals gained a new insight or a new idea. Learning occurs when they can produce the insight or design and can also produce new consequences from the insight.

I believe that making action part of learning is one reason that we observe almost no forgetting curve. Individuals, for example, who learn to reduce their skilled incompetence do not appear to forget these skills because they keep using them. But even when they did not use these skills, they appear not to forget them. They may, as in playing tennis, get a bit rusty, but with some warming up they are able to reach the skill level that they had achieved.

Outcomes in Organizations in Which Double-Loop Learning Is Occurring

One payoff of learning Model II skills is that you can deal with Model I defense routines without being drawn into them, or without having your button pushed. You can reduce the number and length of meetings because you can introduce a degree of openness that helps reduce defensive routines in the first place. Of, if such routines arise, you know how to use them to help individuals learn and grow. You become, to the people with whom you work, what individuals like myself are to the executives whom I have tried to help (recall chapter 2).

Learning Model II skills and using Model II virtues judiciously can help reduce the likelihood that defensive routines would be bypassed and covered up.

Now, let us consider some examples of changes in the status quo. Recall that the organizational defensive pattern is self-sealing and anti-double-loop learning. It is against surprises and rare events. Altering features of such a pattern is therefore a rare event. Here, I want to focus on the rare events that have occurred in organizations in which individuals have become skilled at double-loop learning. In all cases, the rare events resulted in significant accomplishments that people had predicted would probably not occur. In all cases in which they did occur, they became stories and legacies that members of the organization used to illustrate, to expand, and to legitimize progress.

- A case team of senior consultants examined their performance. They discovered that it was less than they desired because of the self-protective actions that individuals of the case team (especially the stars on the team) took to deal with their busy schedules, as well as to deal with the unwillingness of some junior people to speak up about poor performance, their own and that of others.

  The team members worked hard at flushing out all the causes of their less-than-desired effectiveness. Next, they developed an action map of the defensive routines. They used the map in several ways. First, they designed a workshop to help produce the skills and the group norms in order not to repeat the errors. Second, they circulated the map throughout the office and asked for modifications and additions. This was an important educational experience for individuals not involved on the team. Third, the map became part of the educational program designed to teach members how to build effective teams. For the first time the undiscussables of team building became discussable.
- The senior partners met to discuss the poor performance of one senior partner. They eventually concluded that he should leave the firm. During the discussion they also arrived at a design on how to part company. The point here is that the senior partner in question was involved throughout the discussions. As the other professionals learned about what had happened, they concluded that top management really meant that excellence would be the standard. This conclusion left some professionals reassured and some anxious. "If they are tough on themselves, they will be tough on us."
- In a firm that had been started by an entrepreneur, the other

senior partners concluded that the founder wanted to be in control over such activities as hiring new professionals, the compensation schemes, ownership plans, and new directions of the firm. Issues such as these are usually discussed privately. In this firm, they became discussable. It took a half dozen sessions over several years for the firm's founder to communicate that he no longer wanted all that responsibility and slightly longer for the other partners to see how they had been setting up the founder. As long as they believed the founder did not wish to let go, they could let him do all the key firm-building work while, at the same time, insist that they were helpless to change the situation.

- In a large management consulting firm the process for firing a younger consultant was to build up evidence until the officers felt they had a sure case. Then the partner took the candidate to a fine restaurant and fed back the negative decision. At the same time, the partner offered very generous separation arrangements, including help in finding another job. Finding the consultant another job was not difficult because the firm was known to hire consultants of the highest quality and to maintain very high technical standards. Other firms were more than willing to hire alumni of this firm.

  Under the new management, the officer told the prospective candidate of his or her status early. "At the moment, it is our belief that you will have difficulty in making it. We are telling you early because we want to check our attributions with you. Maybe our data are wrong or incomplete, and maybe they are not. We also want to design with you a series of actions that you agree would disconfirm our conclusions."

  The results were encouraging. For example, one young consultant felt that the data used were valid but incomplete. He felt that one officer and a manager in another office in which he had been located for several years would provide different evaluations. The partner encouraged the consultant to arrange a meeting during which this positive evaluation could be accomplished. The meeting was held with the officer and the manager present. Neither supported the consultant. Both said that they were not as positive about his performance as he recalled. Under questioning by the partner, they admitted that they probably had not been as forthright with the consultant in the past because they did not want to upset him. They had been in the dilemma of giving him the bad news in a way that they thought he would hear it. They now realized that they had to be much more explicit and less easing in. The partner then asked the

> consultant if he wanted to design some other actions because he had not received valid feedback in the previous office. A frank discussion, managed by the consultant, ensued. He concluded that he did not wish to continue but wanted help finding a new job.
>
> The request was granted immediately. Again, the corridors were somewhat aghast when the consultant told his friends that the session had been fair and that he had decided to leave on his own volition.

Admittedly, these examples are rare. But the purpose of discussing them here is to indicate the potential of the approach. Admittedly, achieving these results takes time.

However, you do not have to wait until individuals are skilled at Model II in order to get important payoffs. With the help of a skillful professional it is possible to put in place basic policies and practices that simultaneously produce more effective performance and increase the likelihood of future double-loop learning.

I should like to illustrate by an example of defining job duties and responsibilities. One of the most basic tasks in building an organization is for individuals to be clear about their responsibilities and duties. This clarity is usually accomplished by developing job descriptions so that everyone knows who is doing what.

This practice makes good sense, but, especially for upper level and professional jobs, this is a single-loop solution. It is a single-loop solution because it is difficult to write a job description that covers everything; indeed, if you did, the document would be unwieldy, *and* it would probably overlap with other people's turf. The keys are to define the core of each job and to permit the other features to be negotiated as problems arise. But for this procedure to work, there must be a relatively high level of trust among the players. All too often, the lack of trust is behind the demand for tighter job descriptions. Low trust has no ending; it can always become lower. The irony is that to deal with that issue by covering it up activates the downward spiral.

High trust also has no ending. It feeds on itself and increases and expands. In order for this expansion to occur, however, the issue of trust has to be dealt with openly and competently. Most individuals bypass it. At best they act as couriers between partners negotiating the best possible wording of the job descriptions so that "everyone is happy." In my experience, this means that the participants can see how, in the wording, it is possible to defend their positions.

I should like to describe how a small architectural and real estate development firm attempted to deal with the issues around job definition in a different way. The firm, known for its high quality architectural and development services, decided to expand its business significantly. The first order of business was to organize more effectively. The need was clear: professionals were overworked; at times, several individuals were working on the same issue; at other times, no one was working on an issue because each person assumed someone else was handling it. The technical people reported receiving contradictory orders from the senior professionals. They also reported that each professional made demands on them with little or no apparent concern for the demands made by other senior professionals. There was a sense of overwork and disorder bordering on administrative chaos. The reason everything worked to produce excellent services was that everyone was committed to expanding the firm, and providing value added to the firm's clients.

The senior professionals decided that they must act immediately to:

1. Define the roles of the different professionals so that everyone knew what each person was expected to do and what each could expect from others.
2. Develop rules, policies, and structures that would be the basics for stability and also for better predictability and reliability of everyone's performance.
3. Conduct more effective evaluation procedures of individuals' performance.
4. Create a more open atmosphere in order to monitor the new structure and rules so that they did not inhibit initiative and innovation.

The senior professionals reasoned that the first steps were to create more order and reduce the disorder; more stability and reduce the instability; more clarity and reduce the ambiguity. This should be done by redefining the basics, such as each individual's job responsibility, the mission of each department, and the relationship of one group to another.

Several consultants were interviewed to help the professionals with their tasks. All but one consultant focused on the presenting problems. The consultants recommended that they themselves interview the players, observe them in action, and eventually produce a set of job descriptions and a new organizational structure. The consultants emphasized that they would involve the relevant players so that the final product was genuinely theirs.

The other consultant began with the working assumption that most players knew more about roles and structure than did the outside consultant. Indeed, he believed that most consultants developed their recommendations based on the information they obtained from interviewing the clients. The reason the outsiders are needed is that they are seen as being objective, as having no axe to grind, as not being caught up in the organization's defensive routines, and as able to produce a report without being bogged down by the personal agendas of individuals.

The consultant also argued that these reasons should not be bypassed by the consulting process. If the clients sought someone who was objective, they must have had difficulty with their own subjectivity. If they wanted someone with no axe to grind, then they must have experienced themselves as grinding their own axes. If organizational defensive routines existed, they should not be bypassed.

The consultant recommended a first phase in which the top group jointly defined their jobs, the new policies, and the new organizational structure and also reduced any organizational defensive routines identified during the discussions. The second phase was to develop the skills and to create the organizational culture that would help them continue to reduce existing organizational routines and also to prevent new organizational routines from arising.

The senior professionals chose the second consultant with whom they would work on the first-order problems and any defensive routines that were causing or exacerbating these problems. They concluded that if they could reduce the latter while at the same time creating a new sense of order, they would be better off in the long run. They were intrigued by the second phase to acquire new skills and were open to doing so. At the outset, however, they were not clear about exactly what acquiring new skills meant.

The discussions about job descriptions and organizational structure that followed produced evidence of organizational defensive routines and of how the new job descriptions and structure would be at risk if the defensive routines were not reduced.

For example, the group was examining a suggestion made by Partner I regarding the role of the two senior partners. The two managers, who were ostensibly to be responsible for managing projects, expressed their concerns:

MANAGER I: I'm afraid that if Partners I and II have the right to enter the process (as they just described it), they will cause the management of the firm to become distorted.

MANAGER II: Yes; their actions can result in a short-circuit of a coherent managerial process. It throws the weight of decision making way out of kilter, I think.

It makes the management of a project very difficult, if not impossible. It usually ends up a poorer project.

The managers made dire predictions about the impact of the partners' suggestions. But do these predictions mean that the managers believe that the partners are so incompetent as to recommend actions that will distort the very managerial processes they are trying to strengthen? Or, is the problem that the managers fear that they will be overcontrolled by the partners?

The consultant asked his questions. The managers responded by asserting that the partners were wrong and were not open to this fact.

The partners, in turn, felt unfairly accused. They did not believe that their ideas were *that* wrong, nor that they were *that* closed. Moreover, there were other reasons behind their suggestions, which they covered up because they felt that voicing them would upset the managers.

The partners said:

PARTNER II: You managers fear losing control of the timing of the project; profitability, and billability . . .

Partner I and I worry . . . if we defer to the management of the project, we might lose the thing that we hold dear (the design and implementation of a high quality building in a profitable manner).

We feel like we need to be able to control the process long enough to assure that it is birthed in the right way.

PARTNER I: I am open to trying. We'll have to have rules at the beginning.

Hopefully, I'll get some confidence that the managers aren't trying to pull the rug out from under me, to push me out of my field.

And, they'll get some confidence that I'm not trying to run away with the projects and do things behind their backs.

The managers began to see that the partners had some legitimate worries. They did not want to lose control over some of the firm's key activities. The managers were also worried about losing control over their responsibilities.

Being or feeling out of control was a crucial problem, yet it was not being addressed directly. Indeed, if the consultant had permitted the discussion to continue with the cover-ups, the discussion itself would have gone out of control. Recall the executives in chapter 2. They went round and round in circles; they produced lists, but no decisions.

Whenever groups work hard and produce lists but no decisions, they are making a decision, but the decision is covert. They have decided not to let things get out of control. Their strategy is to present their views and stick to them. At the same time, they understand that other people will do the same. The results are lists and no decision. If the leader makes a decision, he or she can then be held responsible for it (a set-up of the leader), and/or the subordinates can complain that they are not given the authority to make decisions (a set-up of themselves and their leader).

The next step was to redesign the roles. The redesigned roles would correct part of the problem. The consultant was interested in helping the managers learn to converse among themselves so that they understood each other more effectively and were able to do so without him. The next step was to redesign the conversations more along Model II reasoning and actions.

This exercise did more than just help the managers to practice Model II skills and reasonings. Watching each other design and redesign their conversations helped all concerned realize that they were all intent on learning the new skills and increasing both the trust and their capacity to learn from each other.

Redesigned Conversation	*Purpose of Redesigned Conversation*
MANAGER I: On the one hand, Partner I, I do not wish to prevent you from talking to others; on the other hand, I should like to illustrate with some examples some of the fears that I have and get your and others' reactions.	Show understanding of partner's possible concerns. State own position and encourage inquiry into it.
MANAGER II: The doubt that I have is related to your commitment to a managerial process. Because you are beginning, it is likely that you may violate the structure and the rules in ways that are counterproductive to the program. These fears I have may be unfair in your mind. I'm open to discussing them.	State own doubts and make them discussable.
I don't know how to confront Partner II or you in ways that we can learn from the violations. At best, I think I feel free to tell you—but as you can see from this conversation—my automatic reaction is to tell you how wrong you are and how we must constrain you.	State that the reason for own fears is the likelihood that you, as well as they, can inhibit learning from deviations.
MANAGER I: I realize the dangers of using a structure and rules to protect us (the managers), but I do not know how to carry out my job without the security of the structure. I am willing to try to design modes with which all of us can agree.	State that you understand the fears that the others have. Also state that you do not know how to have the control that you need without the structure. Express willingness to design jointly.

Redesigned Conversation	*Purpose of Redesigned Conversation*
PARTNER I: Let's take some examples of your worst fears and role-play them to see what I would say and how you would react. Let us see if with the consultant's help and our own, we can develop a greater sense of trust in our own competence to integrate.	Express willingness to describe the fears you have by role-playing them. Also ask for help to improve trust and integration.

Turning to the fears the managers had about the partners' behaving in ways that would cause the managers to get out of control, we hear:

PARTNER I: If I hear you correctly, you are concerned about how genuinely open I will be about my ability to reduce my fears of the rug's being pulled out from under me, etc.	Shows that you understand the source of other person's fears.
Why not pick some examples and let's try them out. I may find that I am not as open as I espouse; or that I vacillate, etc. You may find similar problems.	Suggests exploring some examples and acknowledges that he may act in ways that confirm some of their fears.

The results of this exercise were interesting. One manager left the firm because he realized that he did not want to be a team player. He was an individual contributor and wanted to be left alone. He left, however, without the view with which he began, namely, that the owners were at fault. Another manager eventually left because he could not produce at the high level of quality expected of him in the enlarged job he was given. New managers were brought in with the use of a more rigorous selection procedure. The firm was on its way. It developed core job descriptions and the beginning capacity to deal with problems of trust in a face-to-face manner.

Conclusion

The way to reduce the organizational defensive pattern is to interrupt it in a way that it cannot maintain itself. In order to accomplish this, skilled incompetence, organizational defensive routines, and fancy footwork will have to be interrupted to show exactly how they are counterproductive.

But human beings will not be able to see what they should interrupt, they will not be able to diagnose the counterproductive consequences correctly if the way they think about and construct their reality is consistent with Model I. Human beings can read books like this one and understand the message. But they are unlikely to reduce the defenses without first learning Model II and making it a part of their theory-in-use. Once they do so, they automatically use productive reasoning; they automatically go for double-loop learning; they automatically reflect on what they have been taking for granted, especially around the organizational defensive pattern. That necessarily means that the organizational defensive routines, fancy footwork, and malaise will have to be addressed. Unless they are reduced, the Model II theory-in-use and social virtues are not likely to persevere. Thus, the individual and the organizational factors must be changed in order for the theories-in-use to be deterred early on during the change process.

Reference

Putnam, Robert W., and Dolores Thomas. 1988. "Organizational Action Map: Pay and Performance," in Robert W. Putnam, "Mapping Organizational Defensive Routines. Mimeographed material, Harvard Graduate School of Education, Human Development.

Chapter Seven

Making the New Theory of Managing Human Performance Come True

▶ During the past several decades, a new theory for managing employees has been developing to the point at which it is now acknowledged as being fundamentally different from the traditional theory. This chapter shows that the new theory of management is consistent with Model II theory-in-use and social virtues. The chapter also shows that without using these concepts, management is likely to limit the ultimate effectiveness of the new theory of managing human beings.

The new theory advises movement away from unilateral control, dependency, and submissiveness and toward involvement and commitment (Beer and Spector 1985; Hall and Goodale 1986; Lawler 1986; Walton and Lawrence 1985; Tichy 1983).

Walton (1985) has identified eight policy components of the commitment perspective, four of which are mentioned here. The first component is job design. The emphases are on individual responsibility extended to upgrading system performance, on job design that stresses the whole task and combines doing with thinking, on teams as basic accountable units, and on flexible definitions of duties.

The second policy component is performance expectations. The emphasis is on defining work objectives that realistically challenge and stretch each employee's abilities and energies. The third component is the flat organization structure, where coordination and control are based more on shared goals, values, and traditions, where the emphasis is on problem-solving and expertise, and where the hierarchy is minimized as a way of getting things done.

Compensation policies to create equity and to reinforce group achievements, such as gain sharing and profit sharing, represent the fourth component. Assurance that participation will not result in command requiring individuals to be dependent on and submissive to their bosses.

Notice the frame we are constructing. We are examining the degree of fit or match between the organizational requirements and the requirements made of individuals. Can individuals go along with these psychological requirements? The answer is, of course, if they agree to do so. But if they did agree to do so, they would be agreeing to some self-limited and self-denigrating features. Moreover, the employees who would experience these consequences most would be those whom management would classify as above average.

What is it about human nature that makes these requirements self-limiting and denigrating to the best people? The literature on human development tells us how infants grow to adults. All infants start life with few and limited abilities. Infants live in a world in which they are dependent on and submissive to their parents or whoever is bringing them up. In most cultures, infants are required to move toward having many abilities, some of which they develop in depth. Being an adult also means striving to become relatively autonomous.

The point here is that the changing of command and of task specialization permits work conditions that produce dependency and submissiveness and the use of a few of the more limited abilities. For so much per hour, good benefits, and security—please be a good infant.

Individuals who prefer infantlike conditions will find these requirements tolerable, if not satisfying. Individuals who aspire toward more adultlike conditions will find these requirements frustrating and not satisfying. The former will snuggle up; the latter will feel conflict and tension.

This is why the traditional theory of management is especially self-limiting with employees who seek to use more than their hands, who prefer initiative and growth, who are willing to take excellence seriously.

The way these incongruities are worked out varies with individuals. Indeed, it even varies with each individual as he or she changes over time. It also varies with the kind of work world the organization is willing to create and with the kind of control it is willing to use. This is where the new theory of management comes into play. Its primary requirement is what researchers have called *psychological success.*

Lewin, Dembo, Festinger, and Sears (1944) developed the concepts of psychological success and psychological failure. They showed that the amount of psychological energy people had for any task was strongly influenced by the degree of psychological success and failure they experienced. The more the psychological success, the more energy was available. Indeed, the psychological energy available could outstrip the physiological energy. The conditions of psychological success and failure are consistent with the adultlike conditions, especially at the lower levels of hierarchies. They aspire toward work conditions that are akin to infancy.

Human beings have found ways to cope with this incongruity. One way is to take time off—for example, absenteeism and/or sick leave. Second, they leave their work psychologically but are present physically—for example, apathy, indifference, and/or goldbricking. Third, they can take on an orientation that is the mirror image of the one embedded in the traditional management theory; for example, they can see how much they can get with as little effort as possible.

A fourth reaction develops over the years. Human beings come to accept dependency and submissiveness as long as they are economically secure. They come to believe that if the company cannot guarantee security, then the government should. Hence, the employees seek governments that create political environments that are paternalistic as the best organizational environments.

A fifth way to deal with the incongruity is for employees to reduce their dependence and submissiveness by creating or joining unions. Unfortunately, as far as the kinds of causal factors I am describing, joining a union is the equivalent of jumping from the frying pan into the fire. The employees find themselves now dependent and submissive to a new hierarchy. True, a few unions are beginning to change. My impression, however, is that the unions are still concerned primarily about economic benefits. Their theory of inducements of motivation and control of behavior is inconsistent with traditional management theory.

I am not downplaying the importance of wages and job security. I am suggesting that union leaders realize that there are increasing numbers of senior managers who also value paying high wages and providing job security. Moreover, these more enlightened executives also believe that in order to obtain the productivity required, they should pay more attention to creating work worlds consistent with adulthood and psychological success. To the extent that these two intentions are successfully combined and integrated, the traditional trade union's basis for existence—namely, that management cannot be trusted—will be eroded.

One explanation for the current revolution in management theory is that executives are increasingly realizing that there are important sources of energy and initiative if work is designed to take into account more adultlike features as well as features that are consistent with psychological success.

But how can the new theory of management become self-limiting? In theory, it cannot if it is implemented well. In order for it to be implemented well, new job and work designs will have to be invented, new reward systems put in place, and new educational programs developed.

If you read books such as those cited at the outset of this chapter, you will find, I believe, that they pay little attention to how to deal with such issues as skilled incompetence, organizational defensive routines, and fancy footwork. Unless these issues are dealt with, the potential of the new theory of management could be limited.

The reason we must pay attention to features of the organizational defensive pattern is that implementing the new theory of management can lead to an increased potential for embarrassment or threat on the part of managers and employees. For example, the managers may find the employee initiative that is unleashed difficult to control; they may become threatened; and they may revert to the old theory of unilateral control. The likelihood that these responses will occur during the transitional stages is very high if for no other reason than that we know so little about implementing the new managerial philosophy in every individual situation. As is true with any social innovation, there is going to be a lot of experimenting that may produce embarrassment or threat to the managers.

For example, Kanter (1986) predicts that the new model of management will bring on new dilemmas and contradictions. For example, merit pay will give way to more aggressive pay-for-performance policies. Gainsharing will place more emphasis on group rather than on individual performance; innovation will move toward extreme measures, such as creating new departments; and increasing tensions will arise between command and mutual adjustment systems.

Walton (1985) describes examples in which managers develop production forecasts without involving the employees. The forecasts turn out to be incorrect. When questioned by the employees, the managers denied that they were doing anything wrong. The employees held the general manager responsible. They also attributed to him that he was closed and inflexible. The outside change agent did not agree with their attribution. The workers never tested their attributions.

Lawler (1986) provides many examples from his own and others' experiences. He writes:

> Implementation of many ideas suggested by work groups proves to be difficult for several reasons. It often requires middle-level

managers and staff support groups (such as engineering and maintenance) to implement change or to accept changes in procedures and practices that they developed and that are under control. Not only does this mean extra work for them, it often implies that they have not done their job correctly in the past.

In one change effort, a quality circle focused on the purchase of new trucks for the organization. After months of study an extensive set of specifications was developed. They promised to save the organization hundreds of thousands of dollars by buying trucks that were both easier to maintain and more effective. There was great resistance from the purchasing agent and the industrial engineer to changing the specifications, even though top management approved the idea. It literally took months to get them to change the specifications. By the time the specifications were changed and the actual trucks were purchased, the group had long since disbanded in discouragement, convinced that management was simply engaged in a sham exercise to keep them quiet. Unfortunately, the experience with truck purchasing is typical. (p. 55)

After individuals work for a while on an enriched job, they may come to see themselves differently and to expect much more from the organization. It is not uncommon, for example, to find individuals who, after mastering an enriched job, raise the obvious question of "what's next?" They seek new career tracks, additional tasks, and additional training. All of this calls for significant changes in an organization. (p. 96)

Supervisors are often threatened by their new relationship with their subordinates and sometimes behave in ways that take away the autonomy and freedom that the enrichment program was designed to give to their subordinates. To a substantial degree, they feel threatened with the loss of their own jobs because their tasks have been transferred down in the organization while nothing has been done to enrich their jobs. Ultimately, they may resist job enrichment and systematically de-enrich their subordinates' jobs in order to protect and maintain their own work and power. (p. 97)

At some point in the history of most plant start-ups, whether new-design or not, intense pressure for production develops. The pressure stems from the need to get the plant on-line in accordance with a predetermined, often unrealistic, production schedule. This period has proven to be particularly crucial in the life of most new-design plants. Managers tend to revert back to traditional management practices in times of crisis. They jump in and try to take charge.

> Needless to say, such an act can be very damaging to the successful start-up of the new-design plant. It communicates to everyone that the new principles of management apply only when things are going well. Not all new-design plants get through this period with their commitment to participative management intact. In one instance, start-up problems, many of which were not related to management approach (for example, construction errors, such as building the ventilation system backwards in a sterile drug plant), led the plant manager to declare that the participative-management program was officially abandoned. Many problems stemmed from the fact that no preparation had been made to deal with the necessity for making some decisions, particularly technical ones, in a nonparticipative way. (pp. 186–187)

In a recent study of democratization of seagoing vessels, Schrank (1983) reports that some employees questioned the genuineness of management's intentions. For example:

> The company is so gung-ho about this whole experiment that if you question it, you're considered uncooperative. (p. xiv)
>
> They pay us. Give 'em what they want. Don't rock the boat. (p. xiv)
>
> There was an ambivalence between authority and democracy evident at meetings. The captain dominated the meeting. . . . (p. 71)
>
> At the head of the table sat the captain, very much in charge. Clearly he was the leader and coordinator of the meeting. He was running the show. . . . (p. 73)
>
> The Oslo Work Research Institute can talk about what they call "democratization" but structurally everything is the same: the master is the master; the chief engineer is the chief engineer; they filter down and find their own little pigeonhole, and I doubt there's any real exchange of ideas between the ranks. (p. 96)
>
> I don't remember any men having any say-so about their jobs. It's pie-in-the-sky to say they abolish the boss's job to give the crew more "independence." (p. 97)

Whenever problems such as these arise, they tend to trigger embarrassment and threat. Consequently, the skilled incompetence and organizational defensive routines become activated. These routines may lead the employees to wonder if management is using commitment and involvement as new ways to control them. Management, in turn, will be equally upset by the employee mistrust and lack of gratitude.

The employees have their own skilled incompetence and defensive routines. They too may find themselves threatened by the new requirements, such as initiative, personal responsibility, and self-monitoring. I have observed, for example, many of the situations Lawlor describes and found the managers to be defensive, as he described. But workers also deal with their defensiveness in a Model I manner. They go after the manager, they play "I gotcha" games, or they may set their managers up by waiting until what they expect to fail does fail and then complain about poor leadership.

My biggest surprise has been the degree of defensiveness on the part of professional yuppies who often espouse Model II theories and the new managerial philosophy with a great deal of passion. In one organization that I have been studying for fifteen years, I found that, at the outset, the subordinates (read professionals) acted with minimal defensiveness primarily because the focus was on changing the actions of their superiors and the policies of the organization. As both were changed, the superiors found themselves with subordinates who had difficulty in dealing with each other with the degree of honesty and toughness required if they were to take over managing themselves and important features of the firm, such as compensation policy, ownership, and long-range strategy.

For several years it appeared that the subordinates were seeking ways not to focus on the difficulties they had in managing each other. This is not to say that the superiors were perfect and that they never made mistakes. They did, but the superiors were much more open to correcting their errors than the subordinates were in recognizing, let alone correcting, their own errors.

As time passed, however, subordinates were promoted, the compensation and ownership schemes took hold, and an increasing number of the subordinates began to realize that the next step was to reduce their own defensive routines. As they began to be more effectively self-monitoring, the superiors began to be less apprehensive and more effective, which, in turn, reinforced the positive relationships among the peers.

I am reminded of the president of Corning Glass Works (Vancil 1982), who designed an innovative and participative process for the divisional managers in which they could have a genuine say in the allocation of financial resources. He eventually stopped the process because the divisional managers were not as tough and inquiry-oriented with each other as he had hoped they would be. The sessions therefore were boring and long. My guess is that the president did not realize that the organizational defensive routines and skilled incompetence would have to be overcome first. I think he believed that because the divisional presidents espoused initiative and involvement, they would gladly take it and become involved if given an opportunity. I have seen these experiments tried by several thoughtful executives. None achieved their potential.

What do we learn from these examples? It is not that these kinds of problems should not have occurred. These problems will occur when management is making changes that are potentially embarrassing or threatening. The lesson here is that the problems were dealt with in ways consistent with skilled incompetence, organizational defensive routines, and fancy footwork. For example:

> When managers and employees disagree, each blames the other; they distance themselves from any responsibility to correct the situation by attributing that the others are closed and inflexible.
>
> When the new changes imply that the existing actions of the players have been wrong, individuals become defensive and the players distance themselves lest they upset others.
>
> It often takes months to make a change because of the bypassing and cover-up strategies.
>
> When employees take on more responsibilities, line management becomes threatened. The latter dig in instead of going upward to acquire new responsibilities. They do not go upward because they believe that this procedure will threaten their bosses. They rarely test this attribution because they fear that even a test could be dangerous.
>
> When crises occur, management reverts to the traditional theory of management. This may be exactly the protection wanted by those employees and managers who have doubts about the new management. Those who are committed may feel a sense of disappointment.

Limiting the Success of Involvement and Commitment Theory of Management

Finally, let us look at an example from the top. The CEO in a world-renowned company concluded that the management at all levels had lost a significant amount of their sense of accountability and initiative for cutting costs. Many managers had developed their own groups and own turf; they paid more attention to their well-being than they did to the organization as a whole.

The CEO and his personnel director concluded that one major cause of this problem was the firm's managerial philosophy. The previous CEO had kept tight control over decisions, including small ones.

Consequently, the management, at all levels, learned to buck decisions upward, to become dependent, and to protect themselves by distancing themselves from the organization as a whole, retreating inward to their own subgroup. The CEO and personnel director also concluded that no matter what programs they developed to turn these things around, none of the programs should reinforce the dependency/distancing pattern. Management at all levels had to be involved.

The CEO and the personnel director decided to attend a seminar for line executives and their top personnel professionals. The objective of the seminar was to help organizations move toward the new philosophy of management described at the outset of this chapter. The faculty were world-renowned leaders in the theory and practice of involvement and commitment as a managerial philosophy.

During the seminar, the CEO and personnel director, with the help of the faculty and participants, developed a plan to begin to change their management organization and make it more participative. In line with the philosophy of the program, they also developed a plan to introduce the plan in ways consistent with creating a sense of ownership by the former management.

A series of workshops were designed. The first workshop included the CEO and his reports. They were placed in small groups to diagnose barriers to excellence in their company. The barriers were shared in a large plenary session. The barriers that concerned the CEO were largely surface. Next, they returned to the small groups and designed strategies to reduce the barriers. They also set milestones that could help them identify how well they were doing. They also defined target dates for completion.

The CEO reported that many managers worked hard to implement their ideas. Although the progress was somewhat less than what he had hoped for, he was satisfied that the barriers had begun to be reduced. For the sake of illustration, let us assume that the program was a success. This question then arises: What kind of a success was it?

I asked the CEO if it was reasonable to conclude that the ideas the subordinates presented during the workshops were largely good ones. He said they were. I asked if it was reasonable to conclude that the subordinates did not have difficulties in producing these ideas. Again he agreed and credited the participative nature of the workshop. "The small groups produced a lot of good ideas."

Next, I asked him, "If it is true that the managers knew these ideas, did you ever consider, in your design, to say to them, 'First, I value what you have done and the progress we have made. In the name of continuing this progress, I would like to reflect on what has happened to see if there is more that we can learn. What is it that I do or the company does that makes it necessary for me to take the initiative to identify the barriers, and to design a workshop to reduce them, when you knew the barriers, and you knew how to reduce them?' " The CEO replied that he had never thought of such a question, nor had the faculty and the other participants.

Asking my question was never part of their design. Yet this question goes to the heart of the dependency/distancing problem.

I asked the CEO how he would have felt about asking the question. He replied that he liked the question but would have been hesitant to ask it because "The question might make some of them feel defensive."

I would agree that the question might make some of the immediate reports feel defensive. But if the source of the defensive feelings were that they would have to examine their automatic dependency/distancing activities, then perhaps the defensive feelings should not be bypassed. Indeed, the reason for the defensive feelings might be a sense of embarrassment due to realizing that being in a dependent/distancing mode violated their sense of managerial stewardship. If this were so, then such defensive feelings would be a sign that they were involved and not distancing.

There is a sense in which the question could lead the subordinates to feel trapped. If they felt this way, the trap could be of their own making. If so, the very exploration of it would be an important step forward. If they did not feel trapped and could show that organizational factors were the causes, including the CEO's behavior, that, too, would have been important progress in reducing the dependency/distancing syndrome.

To put this in another light, the way the workshops were designed not to include the "how come" question, lest the participants feel defensive, is itself a bypass and cover-up. Such actions are distancing ones. Ironically, such actions mean that the top management is being managed by the discomfort they believe the reports will experience.

The Tension between the Two Sets of Managerial Models

The consequences that follow from the control and commitment managerial models are different. The first consequence is consistent with unilateral control, power with position, the manipulation of people through activities (such as self-inflicted crises), and the private evaluation of individual performance in order to take action. On the other hand, the commitment model emphasizes bilateral control and mutuality, power with competence or expertise, the motivation of people through internal commitment, and the public testing of performance evaluations before conclusions are reached.

Resolving these differences requires making discussable the values and assumptions embedded in each orientation. For example, the control orientation encourages the values of win/don't lose, of unilateral control over the other people, of suppressing negative feelings, and of acting rationally. Yet these values are not likely to be helpful in the transition stage because individuals are likely to become upset. Plans and implementation are unlikely to be clear and rational, especially because so little is known about how to get from here to there efficiently. Attempts to monitor the new designs with the old values of unilateral control and win, do not lose, are so contradictory to the values of mutuality and cooperation emphasized by the commitment model that the credibility of the entire program can be placed into question.

How did the OD professionals deal with the tough issues just described? Their responses varied with the phases in which they found themselves, as well as with the cooperativeness of the line.

Dealing with Supportive Line Managers: Phase I

The OD professionals reacted to supportive line managers in three different ways. The first reaction was to accept the support and build on it. The second was an initial reaction of disbelief. The professionals doubted that the line managers could be that cooperative. However, they did not state these doubts. They moved toward the third reaction, which was to call them "great clients" and to join with them in the challenge ahead.

In other words, the reactions to the "great clients" were (1) to express gratitude, (2) to hide the disbelief and act as if not hiding it, and (3) to sign them up. Once signed up, the OD professionals probed the line managers diplomatically for negative views that might exist below the surface. For example, the OD professionals often tested their concerns by asking the line managers to specify their commitment in terms of what they would do in actual, specific situations. The line managers tended to find such requests helpful. They saw the OD people as getting down to cases. They did not realize that they were being tested covertly.

Dealing with Doubtful Line Managers: Phase I

How did the OD professionals react to line managers who expressed doubts and fears? Initially, they encouraged the expression of these feelings. Sometimes encouraging the expression of doubts backfired because the OD professionals did not have good answers to the problems. They tended not to admit this, but reacted either by assuring the line managers that the issue was solvable or by telling them that they were wrong. The latter response was followed by an assurance that things would clear up for them once they got into the program.

Often, the OD professionals discussed their clients' negative reactions among each other. They often saw the clients as being irrational. They explained this irrationality to themselves by attributing to clients such qualities as self-centeredness, power orientation, and repression. These qualities all were seen as being natural consequences of the line's control orientation.

Although the OD professionals said that the client's fears were explainable, a diagnosis tantamount to saying the fears are rational (not irrational), the professionals were rarely observed to deal with these issues openly with the clients. The OD professionals tended, at this time, to sell harder by asking the clients to suspend disbelief temporarily and "trust us."

If strategies like these did not work, the OD professionals would then ask the clients to come up with better suggestions. The most difficult clients were bypassed on the grounds that they were not ready.

The consequences of this action were to reduce public discussion of doubts and to increase the cover-up of doubts by both line and OD as well as the cover-ups of the cover-ups.

Dealing with All Clients: Phase II

The second phase dealt with the reeducation of the line managers. Although each reeducation program differed in each organization, all of the programs appeared to have three underlying characteristics.

The first characteristic was an orientation or introduction to the logic of the programs (Nora, Rogers, and Stranny 1986; Perry 1984). The orientation programs were usually in the form of lectures, films, slides, and discussion techniques, all designed to inform the participants. For example, in one program the participants were educated into such concepts as guiding principles (purpose, mission, objective), goals, and the importance of fit among such factors as people, jobs, organizational structure, reward systems, and information processes.

The second reeducation program characteristic was the introduction of concepts that were supposed to capture the heart of the new ideas and values—such as visioning, purposing, ownership, and energy. The meaning of these concepts varied only slightly in the different programs.

Yet these concepts were disconnected from action, although they were supposed to be action-centered. For example, a *vision* was defined as a statement that mobilizes human energy by virtue of its power in describing the unique or distinctive contribution the organization chooses to make to the overall success of the business. When I asked the OD professionals to give examples of visions that mobilized human energy, they were unable to do so. They spoke about visions with energy and fervor.

They had difficulty, however, in defining the core features or properties of a vision.

One cause of this difficulty was the advice given to the participants on how to create a vision. The advice included to (1) fantasize an ideal goal, (2) list activities that turn you on or off, and (3) identify things you want to accomplish and want to be able to say about your work, job, or work place. How clear are managers and employees on these issues? How does one organize the responses into an integrated whole that is the vision that mobilizes human energy? The OD professionals had difficulty answering these questions.

Another example of the disconnectedness is illustrated by the visions created by a plant manager. They were

> never ship a bad product—100 percent quality yield. Goodness is how few people we use. All employees understand our business, our competitors, our goals, and our performance. Plant runs . . . with minimal inventory. No raw material inspection. Positive attitude toward job and area. Fun place to work. (Perry 1984, 13–15)

The reaction of the OD professional to these visions was "These are super" (Perry 1984, 13). As used, however, they could be carried out under a control or a commitment model of management. The plant manager, in effect, raised the ante but did not as yet have the ability to produce these visions consistently with the commitment model. The result was that visions such as these became vehicles to provide unilateral goals to pressure the lower-level employees (Perry 1984).

The third reeducation program characteristic was the use of either/or concepts when defining their program or when comparing the program with the control model. For example, the control model was often associated with macho, with crises, and with immediate bucks, whereas the OD model was associated with learning, with long-term orientation, and with minimal crises. Yet, many of the new programs were implemented, as we discuss below, with OD professionals and line acting macho, with short-term goals, and, when the program was having difficulties, with finding the individuals who were the bad apples. Moreover, the clients became dependent on the OD professionals. This dependency, in turn, resulted in passivity and a low level of energy for work (Perry 1984, 68).

As the dependence on the consultants deepened, the employees began to have ambivalent reactions to the change programs. On the one hand, they felt that progress was being made as long the consultants were helping them. On the other hand, they realized that the dependence was counter to the commitment model. The employees therefore began to question the long-run credibility of the commitment model.

These reactions, in turn, fed back to reinforce the dependence on the OD professionals. The employees faulted the consultants for not providing them with a total picture. They would ask for the specific steps that they would have to go through, or for road maps (Perry 1984, 72).

But the truth was that the consultants had no such complete road maps. They were working with their clients trying to figure out what should be happening next. Although the consultants often said that they did not have a road map but that they were there to help create one, the employees did not hear or believe them. Indeed, some employees even felt that they were being manipulated by the consultants (Perry 1984, 73).

How can we account for this reaction? First, the employees had gone through hours of orientation programs about the value of the commitment model. They could have concluded that if the consultants were so clear about the end results, then they must have a road map. Second, the employees may have assumed that management would not have engaged in these risky change activities unless they had a road map, at least a map that was more complete than the one being presented to the employees. Third, the employees' dependence on the consultants could have become so strong that they would not hear the consultants' assertion that they did not have a complete road map. What sense does it make to be dependent on someone who does not have the knowledge that the employees require?

When these issues were raised, the consultants would respond by taking initiatives to reduce dependence. Many of the initiatives, however, were in line with the control model. For example, if the employees became anxious about fitting into the new organization they were designing, the consultants would advise them to

> "Get emotional. Stop designing 'for them.' Stop holding back. We want your feelings to color the design." (Perry 1984, 44)
>
> When an employee said, "I'm nervous," the consultant replied, "It's about time. Lead time is dwindling. Customers want results. We can't come up with anything short of 100 percent in the first month." (Perry 1984, 45)

Actions like these had important consequences on the line. Because the actions were consistent with the control model, they could allay the line's fear that things might get out of control. In effect, this assurance bypassed the necessity for line to work through their fears of going out of control. The assurance also encouraged the line to see the OD professionals as holding a control orientation, even though they were urging others not to hold such an orientation.

These consequences could have an unintended impact on those line managers who genuinely wished to reduce the control orientation. They could see that they were feeling secure precisely because the OD professionals remained within the line's defense. Such an awareness is not likely to make the programs or the OD practitioners' capacity to deal with the tough issues credible.

The line, however, cooperated as long as the programs received "good press." Good press meant achieving productive goals on schedule. The line learned not to be hesitant about recruiting the OD people, when needed, to do what the OD people call "s____ work." S____ work consisted of routine activities (such as making sure forms were filled out) or actions to persuade the employees (such as asking the OD people to energize and push the employees into faster production).

The OD professionals reacted to such demands by feeling angry and frustrated. Depending on their anger and frustration, they would see the line managers as being sneaky, irresponsible, and fearful; as lacking in integrity; as having no courage; and as still oriented toward quick fixes. These attributions were rarely shared forthrightly and therefore not resolved.

One unintended consequence of these pent-up feelings was that the OD professionals appeared to be insensitive to the line management's justifiable defensive routines. By justifiable defensive routines, I mean the resistances and defenses individuals could be expected to express when they are moving from control toward commitment and, at the same time, are responsible for getting out the production and meeting schedules. As a result, the line often felt that OD professionals were antiorganization and that they lacked empathy with people who held managerial positions.

In some cases, the line began to become anxious about the long-run consequences of the program. Some even felt that they had been sold a bill of goods or that they had too easily taken on the work of the OD professionals.

To the extent that the line chose to become more resistant, the impact on the OD professionals was that they felt bewildered and, in some cases, betrayed. The line and OD professionals, each in its own way, became more self-protective. This resulted in their both becoming more control oriented, more distancing, and less cooperative; and both reduced their level of aspiration of the extent to which they would approximate the commitment model.

Yet they continued to work with each other. The reason is that much progress could be made on production, inventory, and quality control issues without working through the dilemmas described above. The good results occur because providing individuals an opportunity to use many abilities rather than a few, to think and act, to self-monitor, and to control the immediate job are so powerful that they can overshadow the difficulties. However, this success will be temporary, because pressure, manipulation, and distancing increase; and as the second-generation problems involved in implementing the commitment model appear, then the issues will no longer be bypassable.

How OD Professionals Reinforce Organizational Defensive Routines

Introducing the commitment model in a world dominated by the control model requires that important values and behavioral differences be resolved. The control model emphasizes short-term rewards, crisis orientation, quick fix, and covert evaluation. The commitment model emphasizes long-term rewards, problem-solving before crises arise, overt evaluations, and major responsibility for success on systems and groups.

OD professionals dealt with doubtful line managers by asking them to suspend disbelief and to trust them while at the same time attributing to them such qualities as self-centeredness, hanging on to power, and repression. The former actions led to client dependence on the OD professionals. The latter led to cover-ups and to cover-up of the cover-ups.

OD professionals attempted to overcome problems by designing and implementing educational programs about the commitment model. The underlying thrusts of these programs were to persuade the clients that the changes were worthwhile and also to deprecate the long-run effectiveness of the control model.

The concepts OD professionals used to convince and persuade were largely not operational. Where they *were* operational, they tended to create an either/or mentality whose validity depended on the people who used it to have the power to call it valid.

The line management eventually realized that the OD professionals would revert to the control model when they got in trouble. That realization reassured the line that the behavior of the OD professionals would never get out of hand, because the line still placed its trust in the control model if and when crisis occurred. It also led the line to push OD professionals toward actions that the OD people called "s___ work" yet that got them good press and kept them working.

OD professionals became increasingly angry at and frustrated with the line manager. These feelings were mostly censored lest the line become angry and kill or reduce the program.

All the consequences fed back to reinforce the differences that existed in the values and behavior of the two models. Hence, we have a set of self-reinforcing organizational defensive loops.

How do we explain progress toward the commitment model that has occurred so far in the organizations studied? One explanation is related to the changes created by redesigning the work. Such changes give employees an opportunity to experience a higher probability of psychological success and conditions consistent with being an adult. These consequences should lead to the performance results reported so far in the literature. Another explanation is related to the redesign of compensation schemes that reward performance more directly. Under these redesigned schemes, employee work groups that perform well should gain financially. This good performance should be expected to continue as long as the local leadership acts consistently with the commitment model.

There is a dilemma embedded in these consequences. They work as long as the work groups can be left alone and not encumbered by the larger organization. Yet, the commitment model seeks to encourage interdependence among units, galvanizing them into a whole. My prediction is that the organizations will have to overcome the consequences of skilled incompetence and the organizational defensive routines if the expanded hopes are to materialize.

I also predict that these conditions will have to be overcome if the new programs are not to be under a cloud of doubt and threat. If the management agrees to the changes precisely because the movement toward the commitment model can be localized to the people at the lower levels, then there is always the lingering concern that if the new ideas encounter unforeseen difficulties, the top management may clamp down on their implementation.

Conclusion

The new ideas of managing human performance will be greatly facilitated by educating human beings in Model II and Model II social virtues. This education will lead to a decrease in skilled incompetence, defensive routines, and fancy footwork and ultimately to a decrease in malaise.

It is especially important to begin the reeducation at the top and move downward because the top can show that it is able to behave consistently with Model II. This does not mean that Model I is fully replaced. Model I may be a respectable theory of action to use when dealing with routine, easily performed, and programmed actions to produce single-loop learning. Needless to say, professionals should also be educated to make Model II a part of their theory-in-use. They are the ones who espouse theories of action that are consistent with Model II. So far, the majority of senior professionals whom I studied revert to Model I the moment their ideas are confronted by line managers.

Fortunately, as we have seen, and will see more of in the next chapter, double-loop learning for individuals and organizations is doable.

References

Beer, Michael, and Bert Spector. 1985. "Corporatewide Transformations in HRM." In Richard E. Walton and Paul R. Lawrence (Eds.), *HRM Trends and Challenges.* Boston: Harvard Business School Press, 1985, 219–253.

Hall, Douglas, T., and James G. Goodale. 1986. *Human Resource Management.* Glenview, Ill.: Scott, Foresman.

Kanter, Rosabeth Moss. 1986. "The New Workforce Meets the Changing Workplace: Strains, Dilemmas, and Contradictions in Attempts to Implement Participative and Entrepreneurial Management." *Human Resources Management,* 25:4, 515–537.

Lawler, E. E. 1986. *High-Involvement Management.* San Francisco: Jossey-Bass. Reprinted with permission of the publisher.

Lewin, K., T. Dembo, L. Festinger, and P. Sears. 1944. "Level of Aspiration." In J. M. Hunt (Ed.), *Personality and Behavior Disorders.* New York: The Ronald Press.

Nora, John, C. Raymone Rogers and Robert Stranny. 1986. *Transforming the Workplace.* Princeton, N.J.: Princeton Research Press.

Perry, Barbara. 1984. *Enfield: A High Performance System.* Bedford, Mass.: Digital Educational Services Development and Publishing.

Schrank, Robert. 1983. *Industrial Democracy at Sea.* Cambridge: MIT Press.

Tichy, Noel M. 1983. *Managing Strategic Change.* New York: Wiley.

Vancil, Richard F. 1982. "The Corning Glass Case." *Implementing Strategy: The role of top management* (Videotape 179–074). Boston: Division of Research, Harvard Business School.

Walton, Richard E. 1985. "Toward a Strategy of Eliciting Employee Commitment Based on Policies of Mutuality." In Richard E. Walton and Paul R. Lawrence (Eds.), *HRM Trends and Challenges.* Boston: Harvard Business School Press, 35–65.

Walton, Richard E., and Paul R. Lawrence. 1985. *HRM Trends and Challenge.* Boston: Harvard Business School Press.

Chapter Eight

Getting from Here to There

▸ There are several ways to help individuals and organizations overcome skilled incompetence, organizational defenses, fancy footwork, and malaise.

Appreciation Learning Experiences

The first mode provides individuals from any organization with insights into their theory-in-use and into any discrepancies from their espoused theory, as well as into the causes of their unawareness of the discrepancy. It also provides the individuals with an appreciation of how they may be personally responsible for creating the defensive pattern that they decry in their organization. Finally, it provides insights into the varieties of organizational defenses that exist in the organizations represented by the participants in the seminars.

The method is simple in design. It requires professional assistance for individuals who have never experienced it. Each participant completes a case, ahead of time, similar to the kind of case described in chapter 2. The participants discuss each case. They act as consultants to the writer to help him or her become aware of his or her effectiveness and to begin to design new ways to solve the problem described.

Each session is tape-recorded for several reasons. In addition to focusing on helping the case writer, there is a focus on how the others are doing the helping. They get important insights into any discrepancies between their espoused theory and theory-in-use by reflecting on their actions within the group. The tape is given to the individual whose case was discussed so that he or she can listen to it at leisure. Copies can be made for any participant. The only rule is that the tapes cannot be listened to by individuals who were not in the group.

Appreciation and Implementation

The second mode is similar to the first except that all the participants are from the same organization. The learning tends to be deeper because the other participants are familiar with the organization and with the problem written about.

What is even more powerful in this second mode is the learning about the organizational defenses and fancy footwork. For example, senior partners of one of the big eight accounting firms attended such a seminar. The managing partner analyzed the left-hand columns of all the cases to identify the patterns of self-censorship among the top. He concluded that if the top does this kind of censorship, then no wonder they have communication problems. He also noted that the cultural change programs on which they were spending hundreds of thousands of dollars bypassed all of these defensive actions.

Unlike the first mode, the participants spent much time in designing actions to be taken when they returned to their organization. They developed new ways to deal with age-old problems. They also developed the basis for new evaluation and compensation schemes as well as new educational programs beginning with the partners.

Dealing with Actual Business Problems (Away from the Office)

The third mode has groups of participants attend a seminar in which an actual business problem is solved. Cases of the kind described above are written with a focus on the human problems that are likely to have caused the problem or are likely to inhibit the implementation of new ideas to solve the problem.

An example is a seminar for the SBU heads or managing directors of businesses designed to produce next year's strategy (Argyris 1990). The basic theory behind the seminar is discussed next.

Strategy as a Control Activity

Strategy is an activity designed to help executives make their world more manageable. It contains a core set of ideas about how to define the business and victory. It also contains the best analytical techniques with which to analyze the external environment and external capabilities, to generate alternative choices, to identify strategic options, to develop scenarios, and to test options.

The use of these ideas and techniques requires productive reasoning. For example, premises are made explicit, data are collected rigorously, and inferences and conclusions are tested by logic that is not self-sealing.

The Tension between the Technical and Human Theories of Control

We therefore have two theories of how to be in control, especially when the environment is threatening. The technical core ideas of strategy requires that the actors be rigorous and analytical and test their ideas in ways that are not self-sealing. The core idea of Model I is that human beings should deal with threat by defensive reasoning.

The dilemma is that the ideas on how to be in control over embarrassment and threat are themselves embarrassing. The implementation of the human theory of control violates the technical theory of control.

Whenever this occurs, it creates, as we have seen, more embarrassment and threat, which lead to further bypass and cover-up. All of these actions and reactions are highly skillful, and thus actors are often unaware of their impact. Or, if the actors are aware of the negative impact, they blame the organizational defensive routines. They report that they are in a double bind, helpless but to act as they do.

The learning experience was designed to deal with this built-in puzzle and dilemma. The course was designed to teach the best in strategy. The course was also designed to help the participants see how they unrealizingly shoot themselves in the foot (as well as their strategy) whenever they deal with embarrassment or threat. Finally, the course was designed to help the individuals correct these errors *and* learn how to reduce such errors in the future.

The course design included these five elements:

1. The core concept of competitive strategy.
2. The conditions under which the implementation of the concepts would be relatively straightforward.
3. The core concepts in the human theory of control.

4. The conditions under which their activation would necessarily lead to the distortion, if not sabotage, of the strategic concepts.
5. Connecting these four domains of learning with every individual as well as with the actions of these individuals as a team. Helping the individuals become aware of their particular theory of human control and their team's and their organizational defensive routines and of how this theory and the defensive routines tend to hold effective strategy formulation and implementation hostage to designed error.

The First Step: Collecting Data The faculty member who was teaching strategy visited each top management team at their respective locations. The teams outlined their thoughts about the strategic issues they wished to solve. They worked out what knowledge they should produce to bring to the conference center. Several weeks before the session, the teams sent a document to the faculty member, outlining the work they had done and the work they intended to accomplish during the five-day session at the conference center.

At the same time, each team member was asked to write a brief case about an important human problem that he or she would face in implementing the strategy. The completed case was mailed to the faculty member about three weeks before the sessions were to begin.

The Second Step: Strategic Control and Human Theories of Control During the first day, the faculty focused on providing the key concepts of their respective disciplines as these concepts related to the problems inferred from the cases. The first three-hour session was on strategy. The second three-hour session was on organizational defensive routines—how they can lead to limited learning; and how limited learning, in turn, can lead to discussions about strategy that contain gaps and inconsistencies that are either unrecognized or, if they are recognized, are undiscussable.

The Third Step: Formulating and Implementing Strategy and Reflecting on Both Processes Each organic team went into its respective small room in order to begin the work of formulating and designing implementation strategies. When, and if, defensive routines (organizational or individual) arose, they would become a matter of legitimate inquiry.

The examination of the impact of organizational and individual defensive routines occurred faster than expected. For example, Group A began with the general manager's reviewing the strategic thrust that had been developed so far, the questions yet to be answered, and the implementation issues to be discussed, as well as with other issues. After he finished his introduction he asked for any comments.

One executive asked, "Are we to take the ideas on organizational defensive routines seriously?"

> G.M.: Of course; if you recall, I was the one who ended the plenary session by saying they were important. Indeed, I think I called them my nemesis.
>
> EXEC: Yes, I was pleased to hear you say that and I wanted to check to make sure you still felt that.
>
> G.M.: I most certainly do.

The executive then said that in the spirit of making undiscussables discussable he wanted to question the direction of the strategy developed so far. As he continued to speak, it became clear that he was asking for a major change.

The G.M. became very upset and asked, "What the devil is going on? I thought the major directions of our strategy had been agreed upon."

The facilitator intervened to ask the executive what he was feeling and thinking as he heard the G.M.'s reaction. The executive said that the G.M.'s response confirmed his fears. The G.M. wanted individuals to be candid—up to a point. "I think that I may have made an error in raising the question."

The G.M. apologized. He said that he now realized that he was violating what he had espoused in the plenary session and in his first response to the executive's question. "But you know," he said, "it is not easy to hear this." "Yes," responded the executive, "and it is not easy to say so."

The G.M. then encouraged other individuals to speak. Several agreed with the executive. The facilitator asked, "What goes on during these meetings that leads individuals usually to hold back on such data?" The responses were candid. They described several organizational defensive routines about how to go along with a superior when one believes that the superior is wrong but is emotionally committed to his position. For example, "I saw you as wanting this strategy. This is your baby. The strategy makes good sense and thus is not easy to refute it. I figured given your strong commitment and the lack of support that I would get from others, that it made sense to go along. I must say, I did not realize until now that others had similar doubts."

Reflecting on the incident, we see a group describing its own defensive routines that caused several members to withhold technical ideas about strategy. Group members also described defensive routines that prevented them from testing their attributions about what was discussable.

The G.M.'s automatic reactions of dismay and bewilderment were an example of the individual defensive routines. He reacted inconsistently with what he had been espousing, and his reaction was automatic and skillful. As the discussion continued, some group members also became aware of their own individual protective reactions, which were to withdraw and distance themselves from conversations that could be embarrassing or threatening.

The Fourth Step: Examining the Implementation Cases A concurrent agenda was the discussion of the cases that the participants had written. To summarize, the participants became aware of their personal human theory of control, especially of how to make them a poor learner under the conditions in which learning is important. They also became aware of how unaware they were about the discrepancy between their intended outcomes and what they actually produce.

For example:

Participants Believed That:	*Participants Acted as if:*
1. It was important to be candid, forthright, and straightforward.	1. They were candid and forthright in a way that discouraged others from being the same, and they were unaware of this consequence while producing it.
2. It is a good idea to identify error in order to correct it.	2. They were often unaware when they were producing interpersonal errors *and* that they were unrealizingly communicating to other people that they were unaware.
3. It is a good idea to test the validity of their ideas, especially if these ideas were controversial.	3. The tests that were used were weak and often self-serving.

Identifying these consequences in their case-team groups and in their own organic group was itself liberating because most participants believed that these consequences were undiscussable. Examining what made the subjects undiscussable and also what made their undiscussability undiscussable led individuals to make public their private views about what was acceptable behavior in the group and the organization whenever the subject contained potential for embarrassment or threat.

The very discussion of what was undiscussable made it possible to interrupt the cycles that up to this point had been seen as not interruptable. Moreover, the discussion made it possible to define ways not to get into these self-sealing ruts again.

Finally, individuals began to learn how to craft their conversations so that they could act consistently with the new norms and could be helped to see when they were not acting consistently.

All this learning was continually tested against the task of solving business topics related to strategy. Whenever someone wondered "if all this is really necessary" the answer was explored in terms of "if we do not change, then how will we transfer business information that is now inaccessible, ambiguous, and vague into accessible, unambiguous, and clear information?

By the way, once these new norms were created, once ongoing learning was legitimized about reducing the counterproductive features of their personal human theories of control and the organizational defensive routines, then the learning was transferrable, within these groups, to any business subject.

The Fifth Step: Continued Iterative Learning As the week progressed, the boundaries of the technical and behavioral began to become blurred. For example, in several groups, members changed their substantive positions on strategy significantly. They had enough successful experiences in their behavioral sessions dealing with organizational defensive routines that they began to confront issues, in their strategy group, that they had previously covered up.

As they talked about running silent and deep, they surfaced important technical information that changed the inputs into the strategy formulation. By the third day, the integration between the behavioral and the strategic had outdistanced the capacities of the two faculty members. We found ourselves being scheduled during lunch through dinner and into the late hours of the evening.

The Sixth Step: Implementing Their Strategies The groups returned to their respective locations and began to implement features of their strategy.

The Seventh Step: Follow Up The groups returned for an additional three-day session. Several groups had added new members. The faculty designed a mini–crash course in strategy and human behavior. This course turned out to be an error because we shortchanged the new group members. They did not have the in-depth learning that had been available to their colleagues. We decided that the next time we would allocate the appropriate amount of time for such a course.

It is fair to add, however, that the new members were able to learn faster because they were in a group that had developed skills for on-line learning and norms to permit reflection in action.

I should like to highlight two features of these discussions. First, the group members discussed, in a group, what would have been undiscussable a year ago. The sales executives, for example, would have been hesitant to discuss openly, in their group, how blind they had been about the problems of implementation. They would also have been hesitant to admit how the implementation frustrations were leading them to change their minds about the technical strategic thrusts to which they had agreed.

The second feature was a discussion of deeper problems. For example, with the help of the faculty, the CEO and several others were able to say that the reason they were hesitant to take the sales executive's concerns about strategy seriously was that they were attributing to him that he was feeling frightened about the changes. They did not wish to base changes in strategy on reasoning used by an executive they believed was frightened. Moreover, the CEO and the several other group members were apprehensive about discussing such issues, especially because they believed the sales executive was unaware of how frightened or apprehensive he sounded.

The sales executive was indeed surprised to hear this. He insisted, however, that he was not frightened. Indeed, he was apprehensive but not about himself as much as about the impact the new strategy was having on the organization. Having learned from the session, he asked his fellow team members what he had said or done that had led them to believe that he was personally apprehensive. They were able to provide him with concrete examples, which helped him think about how to craft his conversation in order to express more accurately his apprehension about the organization.

Dealing with Actual Business Problems at the Office

There is a lot of talk these days about visions. There was much dissatisfaction in the large corporation in which this learning experiment occurred, especially among the human resources professionals. They were critical of the CEO for not having an adequate vision that they could use to plan their efforts.

The newly appointed vice-president of human resources (VPHR), who was a line officer, had his doubts about the complaints being made. He knew the CEO well and believed that he had written a document on which his department could build a strategy. He also believed that some of the complaining by his staff could be partially a defense of themselves. He wanted to learn if this were so, including if he were wrong.

The VPHR began by asking individuals and groups within human resources about their effectiveness. The overwhelming response he received was that the people and groups did not feel very effective; indeed, many felt disempowered. They placed the responsibilities on the CEO for not having a valid and usable mission for human resources and also on the line management for disempowering the human resources profession.

The VPHR felt that many of the human resources professionals were indeed disempowered. But, recalling his experiences as a line officer, he felt that the line was able to disempower the staff because the staff were not very competent and because they were skilled at permitting themselves to be disempowered. When he raised these ideas as hunches to be tested, many of the human resources professionals interpreted his actions as aggressive and hostile. Nevertheless, VPHR began a series of actions that illustrate the kinds of interventions that I believe are important.

Phase I

The first step was to invite fifty respected representatives of human resources to an all-day workshop. The VPHR began the workshop by stating that the CEO had read the results and wanted to take constructive action. The VPHR suggested to the CEO that he develop his vision for human resources. At the same time, the VPHR would invite a group of representatives from human resources to do the same. The two views would then be compared, and the CEO would be willing to meet to discuss the views. The CEO agreed.

The fifty participants spent the day developing a vision and a missions statement to recommend to the CEO. The group was broken into subgroups. The subgroups met periodically to share and consolidate their views. By the end of the day, the walls were covered with newsprint. A vision and mission statement had been produced. The VPHR asked the group to compare their product with the existing vision and mission statement. After lengthy discussion, the group members reluctantly agreed that their statement was as abstract, vague, and unusable as the one they had criticized. The session ended with some degree of grumbling and dismay. Many members said that they wanted to wait for the CEO's statement.

The strategy of Phase I can be summarized as follows:

1. Acknowledge the participants' diagnosis of an organizational problem.

2. Ask the participants to produce several alternative ways to solve the problem.
3. Use the exercise to raise their awareness of their inability to produce what they had demanded of the CEO and top-line management. Raise the question of how aware they were of their inability.
4. Help them begin to see the gaps, inconsistencies, and self-limiting features of their diagnosis.
5. Raise the possibility that their diagnosis was embedded in organizational defensive routines and that it illustrated their fancy footwork.

A few weeks later, the memorandum from the CEO arrived. The same fifty professionals were assembled to analyze and discuss it. The gist of the CEO's memorandum can be captured in the following statements that he wrote:

> Change is a way of life, not an end.
>
> Remain committed to basic values of involvement, joint participation, and individual responsibility.
>
> Excellence.
>
> Tolerate and expect differences in working practice and treatment.
>
> Above-average pay for above-average performance.
>
> Leader in human motivation.
>
> Push decisions down to where the knowledge is.
>
> Recruit better-than-average employees.
>
> Provide high quality educational experiences and personal development.

The overall reactions to the CEO's memo were a mixture of negative criticism and disbelief. They agreed with most of the list, yet they criticized it as being too abstract. Someone noted that the lists they had created at the previous meeting were just as abstract. No one replied to this observation. Someone then returned to finding fault with other participants, not with themselves. For example, they doubted that line officers would tolerate differences in views, that they wanted genuine participation, and that they would take responsibility for personnel actions. They also criticized the list because it did not include what the CEO believed had to change. The overall attitude was "show me."

The VPHR recommended that the group invite the CEO so that they could have a direct discussion with him. The VPHR said he would be glad to show the CEO their reactions in advance so that the CEO could come prepared to discuss them.

The group became silent and seemed to have lost its bravado. The VPHR asked how he should interpret the silence. More silence followed.

Then, some participants began to talk. The first two said that they liked the idea of inviting the CEO. A third said that he was not in favor of showing their comments to the CEO because their comments were largely negative. Many heads nodded, and several said, "I agree." A second silence occurred; a participant then said that the CEO might interpret the list as a set-up. There was further agreement and further silence.

I intervened twice during this episode to make the following points:

> Why do you frame a diagnosis of the CEO's list in ways that, if you showed the diagnosis to him, you would predict he would feel set up? Let's examine the reasoning that went into making up your diagnosis. You may do this with other people. If so, it could be a partial explanation for line's negative feelings about you.
>
> If you believe that the CEO could experience your list as a set-up, then if you meet with the CEO, how will you deal with that? If you cannot deal with this reaction, then are you not setting up yourselves in front of the CEO?

More silence. Then one participant said, "I do not agree with your points. We said these things here because we were asked to be honest. There was no thought of sharing these views, as stated, with the CEO."

Someone responded, "That's not true. A few of us, me included, agreed that the CEO should see the list."

I intervened:

> It is true that two of you recommended the list be shown to the CEO as is. It is also true that the number of people who want to edit the list to make it more positive is very large and is increasing.
>
> As one of you said, we are not foolish enough to say what we have produced. I would like to ask why you use reasoning and produce a diagnosis that would be foolish to share directly with the CEO?

(later)

If you edited the list to read more positively, could you hide the thoughts and feelings that you censored when the CEO starts to question you?

I then asked, "Do you believe that the CEO could predict the negative features of the list?" Most participants, including the ones who wanted to edit the list, replied yes.

"Then what are we hiding? Moreover, if we do edit these features, will we admit that they were edited? If not, would we then have to cover up that we edited and also cover up the cover-up? And if so, would we not be creating the conditions of disbelief and disempowerment that we have said are counterproductive? Moreover, would not our edited comments be more abstract than the original list?"

Three of the participants agreed and said that they were stuck. A fourth agreed and said that this encounter was typical of human resources professionals. "We chicken out. We tell people to be candid and build trust, and we do neither."

Several other participants created the following line of reasoning:

If we are correct that the CEO would expect the list to be negative,

If we give him an edited list that was not the negative one, and acted as if we did not edit it,

Would he not doubt the validity of the list?

Moreover, might he not take a cue from our cover-up, and cover up his views about us?

More participants began to see the inconsistency in their position. There were about ten, however, who felt that this line of reasoning was making a mountain out of a molehill.

The group finally recommended that the VPHR and his top group should meet with the CEO and discuss the list. They could then report back to the larger group.

Note what was happening. The personnel people were given an opportunity to produce a mission statement. They failed. They were then asked to evaluate the CEO's list. The reactions to this list ranged from "It is too abstract" to "Does he really mean it?" As to the former reaction, their lists were equally abstract. As to the latter reaction, it is an example of trying to place the fault on others. If the list is not credible, then it cannot be taken seriously.

The vice-president offered to invite the CEO to a meeting to discuss the participants' evaluations. After a few agreed, the group backed off.

They recommended that their top personnel group meet with the CEO. Note the fancy footwork. When given a chance to test their attributions, they delegate the task to someone else and cite as the reason that the group is too large.

The Strategy of Phase II

The strategy of Phase II includes the following five steps:

1. Acknowledge the participants' diagnosis of the CEO's beliefs and intentions regarding the human resources function.
2. Provide the participants with an opportunity to compare their version with the CEO's list.
3. Create the conditions in which the participants could react to the CEO's memo publicly. The objective was to help the entire group see the variance in views, the logic embedded in the views, and any defensive routines and fancy footwork that they produced in dealing with the issues.
4. Ask the participants to define the next step that they believe was important.
5. Provide further evidence of their defensive routines and fancy footwork.

The VPHR and his staff met with the CEO. The staff did not send him the list of reactions ahead of time. The CEO, however, came prepared with his own list.

He began by describing what he believed were the concerns of personnel. His list was close to what the large group had said. The CEO reminded them that he had been promoted from within and therefore had many years of experience with personnel professionals. He accepted responsibility for causing some of their problems and asked them to examine their own responsibility for creating the problems. For example:

You Complain	*My Question to You*
You tell me that you are tired of holding the line managers' hands on routine but important personnel requirements such as performance evaluations and grievances. You ask me to produce a policy against hand-holding.	I can write a policy, but I do not believe it is enforceable. There was such a policy when I was a plant manager, and I never followed it. I did my best to delegate my responsibilities to personnel. It was wrong to do so, and you let me get away with it. The way to correct this situation is to correct the relationship that you have with line.

You Complain	*My Question to You*
You say that you are tired of feeling disempowered. You want a mission statement or a vision to reduce the disempowerment.	I cannot produce a better view of the mission than I did with the list that I sent you. I heard that you were not able to produce one that you felt was better. Perhaps the source of your disempowerment lies in how you think and behave.
You complain of the existence of an antipersonnel point of view in this organization.	Many line executives feel that you have an antiline management view.
Some of you say that you are tired of covering up what is on your mind with the line. You want personnel rules and regulations that you can use to change your relationship with the line.	I hope you do say what is on your mind. In my experience, many personnel people do speak their minds. Their problem is that they do not appear to use tough analysis and reasoning when they do so. They back off quickly.
You would like personnel to be in the mainstream. You want a seat at the table.	I want the same thing. The opportunity is there, but you have to earn it. You will not earn it as long as what we have just discussed continues to exist.

After the CEO left, the group continued its discussion. They admitted that the CEO had been candid and forthright and that he had pulled no punches. They also agreed that he was open to being influenced, although a few group members expressed their doubts. They agreed with some of his advice, but not with all of it. They agreed that the next step was for them to reexamine their own operations to see if they could increase their effectiveness.

The Strategy of Phase III

The strategy of Phase III includes the following five steps:

1. Acknowledge the CEO's diagnosis of the problem.
2. Discuss similarities and differences in views.
3. Make explicit the tensions and conflicts embedded in both views.
4. Expose the top human resources officials to the CEO's solutions and have them challenge the solutions however they wish.
5. Ask the human resources officials to identify the next steps, including what they might do to facilitate progress.

Phase IV

During their respective staff meetings, the senior human resources officials communicated what had happened in the meeting with the CEO. Most reported that the CEO had been forthright and open to being confronted. The ball was clearly in the human resources' court.

Although many people agreed with this conclusion, none of the groups took any action. One might say that there was a deafening silence. But this itself was a loud message, and the VPHR permitted it to resonate throughout the human resources organization.

Several months later, he attended a meeting in which the issue of disempowerment of personnel and OD professionals was brought up. The VPHR suggested that a committee be assembled, composed of respected personnel administrators (PAs) and a few respected line officials. The committee would be charged with developing a new role for PAs that would reduce the sense of their being disempowered.

The strategy of Phase IV was to raise the reactions of the human resources professionals to the challenge of taking initiative. The reaction was largely one of silence.

The moment an opportunity arose to continue the process, the VPHR took the initiative. He set up a committee to make recommendations to solve a perennial problem, namely, disempowerment of PAs.

The committee began by making its own list of the causes of ineffective performance by PAs. The list was similar to several others that had been produced in previous meetings.[1]

1. Lack of a clear-cut statement from the top as to the corporate personnel division's mission, which led to a lack of clarity of the role of the PAs.
2. The present roles of the PAs were described as follows:

"We often act as the whores of corporate management. When threatened by line, we back down."

"Line expects us to do the dirty work or the highly detailed work."

"We are expected to do everyone else's job. If it does not fit anywhere, we're expected to do it. Jacks of all trades and masters of all (or none)."

---

1. This phase was conducted by Dianne Argyris.

> "PAs must be politically astute. They must go along with personnel actions that line takes. If they do not, the PAs could get into trouble."
>
> "PAs have a second-class status in the eyes of line management. They are not seen as being central to the running of the organization."
>
> "PAs do not have their own power. They do not believe that they would be backed up by the top personnel officers in a showdown with the line."
>
> "PAs are not receiving a sense of acknowledgment and appreciation that they believe they deserve."

Why don't the PAs deal directly with their line supervisors to solve these problems? Their first reason is that it could be professional suicide to do so. The second reason is that the PAs believe that their superiors would not support them. There is, as we shall see, validity to both observations but for reasons that are different than those stated above. For example, it could be professional suicide to confront the line managers because the PAs are not good at such encounters, and not because of the line's deficiencies. The line may indeed have deficiencies, but they are unlikely to examine them at the request of the PAs if the PAs themselves are not competent in the skills they are asking the line to learn.

The PAs' Recommendations for Solving the Problems

The PAs recommended a new role for themselves. It included these five aspects:

1. To be a change agent.
2. To have more responsibility and an orientation toward process.
3. To be perceived as an integral part of running the business.
4. To play a major role in human resource management, such as training, work-force planning, job design, and career planning.
5. To influence and educate line managers to do more effective employee relations and to be sensitive to situations that require PA involvement.

On the one hand, the PAs recommended that they take on more responsibilities in organizational development and other types of change-agent work. On the other hand, the PAs' own diagnosis suggests that their relationships with line are not conducive to effective change-agent activity. For example, line sees the PAs as being second-class citizens, as not being strong, as not understanding the business, and even as being antibusiness.

There is a more important dilemma. On the one hand, the PAs were ready to stake their credibility on changing the organization. On the other hand, they did not have a track record for changing their own behavior. How would the PAs help line become aware of the line's shortcomings of which they were unaware if the PAs could not help do the same for themselves?

The PAs became dissatisfied with their inability to go beyond their diagnosis and recommendations, which they knew line management had questioned on previous occasions. They wondered if they could produce a new set of recommendations that was more likely to be implemented. We were invited to help the task force answer this question.

We suggested that the first step be to test the validity of the assumptions embedded in their diagnosis. How true was it that the PAs would be more effective *if* line changed their behavior, *if* the human resources people defined a new and more powerful mission, and *if* the top human resources people backed up the PAs more strongly when the latter got into difficulties with the line? The PAs agreed to the suggestions to test these assumptions.

The diagnostic strategy, therefore, shifted to discovering the extent to which PAs were skillfully incompetent in dealing with the line. The vehicle we used to make this diagnosis was a version of a case study approach described in chapter 2.

The PAs wrote their cases and sent them to us. We, in turn, checked them for usability. We then scheduled a workshop. The cases constituted the core of the workshop's curriculum. One key product of this workshop was a map the PAs produced that showed how the ways they acted to solve the problem were counterproductive.

As in the case of the executives in chapter 2, the major lesson that the PAs learned was how they were responsible for their own disempowerment. The group members advised the writer of each case that the strategy and actions described in the case to reduce disempowerment was itself a recipe for disempowerment.

After the first six cases, this diagnosis became repetitive. The group turned to redesigning their conversations. As could be predicted, the group began to see that insight and awareness were not enough. They now knew this; they understood it, but that understanding did not lead them to produce new conversations.

They turned their attention to learning Model II theory-in-use and to producing Model II social virtues. This led them to develop a map, of the same type presented in chapter 7, about the organizational defensive routines and fancy footwork that had led them to disempower themselves. The map graphically represented what they had to overcome. They then recommended a set of seminars for human resources personnel to learn the new ideas and skills.

By the way, the group did not decide easily that their report to their fellow professionals should be, in effect, "We discovered the enemy, and it is us." They were worried about whether they were going to be believed by the other people. They were also worried that the report might produce negative and destructive reaction from the top line executives.

Many of their colleagues found their report compelling. It was full of quotations and descriptions of dilemmas that were reminiscent of what the colleagues themselves usually say and how they usually act when they try to reduce their own disempowerment. The CEO and VPHR were even more supportive. Both made public laudatory comments about the insight and courage shown by the twenty PAs. They promised the resources necessary to continue the reeducative process. The CEO said that, for him, the report helped him jettison a lot of baggage because the report made discussable what hitherto had been undiscussable.

The trend begun by this process three years ago continues. Many PAs and OD professionals have attended seminars in order to reduce their skilled incompetence and the organizational defensive routines. Slowly, they have begun to redesign the courses that they taught (e.g., in leadership, group effectiveness, culture change) so that they could introduce the new ideas and skills they were learning.

Some succeeded better than others. They created groups in which they would meet to help each other continue learning. The perseverance was high; the forgetting was low.

Line and staff people who began to experience the new ideas asked to attend the courses. Some of the more diehard PAs and OD people who resisted the change began to climb aboard. A few tried it out and found it more difficult than they had thought. Several concluded that they could not be effective in the new approach. They were able to discuss their views with other people in the support groups. Those who chose to find different work within or outside the organization were helped to do so.

A team of the graduates of the new program developed the map about pay for performance (chapter 7). Recall that they recommended that if top management decided to bypass the organizational defensive routines, they should say so openly. After several discussions at the top, the CEO concluded that the bypassing strategy was not the preferred one. He also concluded that the top executive group had to examine their own bypassing and cover-up strategies. After two years of work, some human resources officials have begun to earn a seat at the top management table.

How Difficult Is It to Learn the New Concepts and Skills?

If difficult means how complicated are the concepts, then the answer to this query is, not very difficult. Model I and Model II are not new to individuals. Both receive instant recognition. In the case of Model II, individuals do not have to learn a new or strange theory. What is new is that the ideas become part of our theory-in-use.

The reeducative process needed to make this come true also is not difficult. More than anything else the process requires practice. Most of the practice can be done while dealing with important business problems. For example, the CEO and his immediate reports in the consulting firm (chapter 2) began their education and practice while solving their strategic problem, and the young architectural firm while defining job descriptions (chapter 7). The large decentralized company began its education and practice by redesigning its mission (chapter 4).

There appears to be no forgetting curve. Once people learn the ideas and gain the skills, they do not seem to forget them. In some cases in which the people did not use the ideas and skills for months because a new CEO had been brought in, they had little difficulty in getting up to speed when the conditions were ripe.

The key criterion for learning is how open individuals are to examining their personal responsibility, to playing with ideas that seem wrong, and to dealing with their bewilderment and frustration while they are learning.

For example, one senior executive said, "When you showed us the seven errors (chapter 1) I recognized them instantly." I agreed. "Then, when you showed us the revised list, and told me that list of rules had to be in my head if I agreed with the first list, I felt this was ludicrous." In this case the executive was candid *and* was open to a dialogue between himself and myself as well as with others present in the room. As a result, he saw the point and now wanted to see exactly how he used those rules without being aware of doing so. He remained open to further inquiry and experimentation. If he had said, "This is ludicrous," and closed off, then there would have been little learning.

This example illustrates that there are two kinds of defensiveness. In Type I defensiveness, individuals defend their views with vigor *and* they remain open. In Type II defensiveness, they defend their views and remain closed. By the way, the most destrictive form of Type II defensiveness is not when someone says, "I don't believe this," or "I will not believe this." The most destructive form is the type in which the individual insists that he or she is open and correct and that it is the others who are closed and incorrect. The fancy footwork cases in chapter 4 illustrate the most destructive Type II defenses, especially if they are used by senior executives.

The organizational defensive pattern can also lead individuals to opt for Type II defenses. Individuals may feel so helpless about changing their pattern that they react instinctively by closing down.

But all is not necessarily hopeless when this happens. We have often helped management design interventions that get at problems people truly want to solve and do so by involving them in the design and execution of the solution. As one mini-intervention works, they up the ante. Upping the ante is the name of the game.

Conclusion

We are learning that it is possible to overcome organizational defenses. The six steps that have been identified so far are to:

1. *Make a diagnosis of the problem.*
2. *Connect the diagnosis to the actual behavior of the participants.*
3. *Show them how their behavior creates organizational defenses.*
4. *Help them to change their behavior.*
5. *Change the defensive routine that reinforced the old behavior.*
6. *Develop new organizational norms and culture that reinforce the new behavior.*

Reference

Argyris, Chris. "Strategy Implementation: An Experiment in Learning." *Organizational Dynamics*, Winter 1990.

Chapter Nine

Upping the Ante

▸ Organizational defenses can no longer be ignored, especially by bypassing and by covering up the bypass. The only thing worse than having organizational defenses and fancy footwork is denying that they exist. Not only does such denial blind us to what is going on, but it also makes us blind to the fact that we are designing our own blindness.

Organizational denial and the delusions that make it possible to deny the denial can lead to organizations that are strangled by their own defenses. And even that has to be denied.

Practices That Minimize the Organizational Defenses

There are at least two reasons that the negative consequences of these activities build up slowly and, like environmental pollution, take time to surface. First, organizations do their best to minimize reaching the saturation point beyond which the defenses take control. They do this by designing their activities to be easy to implement, easily routinized, and requiring single-loop learning for monitoring them effectively. They hope this design reduces the likelihood of embarrassment or threat.

Second, managers are continually inventing ideas and procedures that detect errors more accurately and that are immune to the human predisposition to distort in order to protect. This development of ideas immune to distortion accounts for the increasing push to make such disciplines as strategy, finance, accounting, manufacturing, and marketing more rigorous. Such rigor, it is hoped, will introduce more productive reasoning into the actions and policies of organization. The underlying assumption is that the more an organization can be managed by the use of disciplines that require productive reasoning, the less likely is the activation of defensive reasoning and the more likely that if it arose, the defensive reasoning could be engaged, if not stopped.

Because all functional disciplines have at their core a set of technical ideas and procedures to accomplish productive reasoning, the theory seems plausible. The problem is that the technical ideas and procedures are not self-implementable. Human beings do the implementing. Once people become involved, they bring with them their capacity for skilled incompetence and the organizational defenses, fancy footwork, and malaise that follow. But none of these are likely to be activated unless the correct implementation of the functional disciplines is embarrassing or threatening. At that point, the defenses will blunt the value-adding potential of the functional disciplines—ironically, at the very moment the organization needs them most.

A second major strategy is being used to minimize the counterproductive consequences of organizational defenses. I refer to the trend to switch the philosophy and practice of managing people away from unilateral control toward involvement and internal commitment described in chapter 7. The underlying assumption of this strategy is to develop players with a higher tolerance of embarrassment and threat. They thus are less likely to activate the skilled incompetence and the organizational defenses.

The strategy of involvement and internal commitment is based on the research suggesting that whenever work taps the actual capabilities of human beings and also activates their potential for growth, human beings will exhibit more energy for work as well as a greater commitment for detecting and correcting error. The problem with this assumption is not that it is wrong. The problem is that this assumption is an incomplete one on which to build a major organizational strategy.

Human beings also show remarkable ingenuity for self-protection. They can create individual and organizational defenses that are powerful and in which that power is largely in the service of poor to mediocre performance as well as of antilearning. To date, the books written about the new management focus heavily on human beings' capacity to be productive and to take initiative. True, these books may alert us to individual and organizational defenses, but they say very little about how the latter inhibit the former.

Several years ago, I interviewed one of the most frequently sought after consultants on job redesign. When I described the negative impact of individual and organizational defenses on the new managerial designs about which he was advising, he recognized these defenses as being real. He said that he warned his clients that it would take a good deal of courage not to permit the defenses to dominate the new designs. The relevant point here is that he had several thick books specifying how to design and implement high performance work systems but only a few pages of admonitions on how to deal with the negative consequences of skilled incompetence and organizational defenses.

Defenses will not prevent all progress toward employee involvement and commitment. Progress will occur until the continued effective implementation activates embarrassment or threat. At that point, if the players have no new skills and the organization no new policies to reward using the new skills, it is possible that feelings of disappointment and helplessness will develop, eventually reactivating the feelings of cynicism reminiscent of the old days. When the feelings about the old days and feelings about the new dream combine, the organizational defenses will increase in strength and will deepen their organizational roots.

A Mind-Set for Upping the Ante

As massive and overwhelming as these trends might be, they are alterable. The learning processes that are being developed are relatively straightforward and easily able to be integrated into everyday practice, do not require so much attention that everything else has to stop, and appear to have the nice feature of a very low forgetting curve. Also, the basic techniques learned to solve a particular problem can be transferred to other problems.

The key is for the players to develop a mind-set that includes these four activities.

1. Players should stop taking for granted what is being taken for granted. They should examine what is not obvious about the obvious.
2. Players should make learning as sacred as encountering no surprises so that they can see how no-surprises policies will likely lead to surprises that are more fundamental and harmful.
3. All players should realize that they are, to some degree, personally responsible for creating, adding to, and maintaining organizational defenses. The players are responsible for diagnosing their contributions and for beginning to reduce the organizational defenses.
4. Players should learn that productive reasoning is as important for human problems as it is for technical problems.

The New Mind-Set and Organizational Inner Contradictions

It is very important to apply the new mind-set to factors that are powerful yet difficult to see until it is often too late. I refer to the inner contradictions that are embedded in the very foundations of managerial theory. One important inner contradiction is that the design presently used to manage organizations rationally will tend to create organizational injustice. Being embarrassing and threatening, this organizational injustice activates the organizational defenses that then lead to irrational consequences. How do we arrive at this contradiction?

Everyone acknowledges that the information used to manage organizations should be valid, timely, and user-friendly. In order for these conditions to exist, the information system designed must take into account the capacities and constraints of the human mind.

Picture a hierarchical organization. At the lower levels of management are first-line supervisors. Next are second-line supervisors, and on up until we reach the top. For the sake of example, I focus here on the nature of the information required by first-line supervisors and by any senior executives.

The first-line supervisors manage a small group of employees. The senior executives are responsible for managing the total organization. Let us call the information system used by the senior executives a distant system. It is distant in the sense that it is far from where the firing line and action are. Let us call the information system used by the first-line supervisors a local system. It is local in the sense that it is close to the firing line, close to where the action is.

Each information system requires different types of information. For example, first-line supervisors of small production groups usually deal with information that is concrete, unique to the group, subjective, and implicitly logical. Within this information, it is difficult to develop trends or to use it for comparison to other groups. The first-line supervisors speak of Mary, Joe, or Bill as the people who work for them. They often describe their subordinates in concrete, emotional, subjective terms. First-line supervisors often become angry with information systems that treat "my people" as categories or numbers. They often resist being compared to other groups because they see their respective groups as unique.

Senior executives, on the other hand, are responsible for the total organization. It is not within the capabilities of the human mind to know all the information of hundreds or perhaps even thousands of groups. It is not possible for the executives to treat each group with its full uniqueness. Indeed, in some instances, such individualized treatment would be wrong because treating one group more favorably than another is the basis for injustice. Senior executives thus require information that is more abstract, objective, and explicitly logical and that is trendable and can be compared.

The effectiveness of the first-line or senior supervisor is directly affected by how well each person uses his or her respective information. Each person develops a different set of skills on how to deal with the type of information he or she must use. The sense of personal competence and confidence becomes directly influenced by how well each uses the different types of information. That means that the first-line supervisor's sense of competence and confidence will be associated with using local information. The senior executive's sense of competence and confidence will be associated with using distant information.

Moreover, the first-line supervisors may view the abstract, objective, distant information systems as unfair, unjust, and inhumane. The senior executives may view requests to think locally as unfair, unjust, and inhumane. We thus have a tension that could lead to embarrassment or threat. Once these forces are activated, we also activate the bypass and cover-up strategies described in this book. Once these strategies are activated, we increase the likelihood that invalid or distorted information will be created or that the timeliness of the information will be reduced. Either or both of these consequences leads to information that is hardly user-friendly.

And so we have a paradox. Information systems designed to produce valid, timely, and user-friendly information may create conditions in which the systems, if used correctly, will produce invalid, untimely, and user-unfriendly information.

Let us reflect on how the argument was made. It began with these premises: there are low-level bosses and high-level bosses. Each level requires information in order to manage. The local information is appropriate for the low-level bosses; the distant information is appropriate for the higher-level bosses. So far, the argument does not appear to create the seeds for an inner contradiction. The contradiction arises when we ask what the likely impact of these premises will be on people's sense of competence and confidence, as well as on what they judge to be fair and unfair. The case for the contradiction gets stronger when we show that the impact could be embarrassing and threatening, which, in turn, could produce counterproductive consequences.

I believe that managers at all levels should learn to do more of this type of reflective thinking in order to alert the organization to the potential counterproductive consequences of actions that at the moment seem rational and straightforward. Without such reflection, organizations will become increasingly filled with activities that are counterproductive and straightforward. But, their straightforwardness is not discussable.

Ethics and the Organizational Defenses Pattern

Andrews (1989) writes that openness and trust are essential to building ethical behavior in organizations. Yet, the contributions of the cases in his book say little about how, if at all, skilled incompetence and organizational defenses helped create the organizational conditions that facilitated (in a less than obvious fashion) unethical actions.

In order for unethical actions to succeed, they must be designed not to see the light of day. We can see this fact clearly when we speak of such acts as stealing and swindling. It is the task of law enforcement to uncover the cover-ups or the loopholes that permitted the intent of the law to be bypassed.

This book is not about the small minority of employees who steal and swindle. It is about the large majority who create and collude in the creation of defensive actions that are also designed not to see the light of day. The cover-up continues for years; it is taken for granted; it is as natural as the fact that night follows day. The result of these countless everyday actions is to deaden individuals' awareness to the ethical pollution they are producing.

My generation never realized that we were contributing to the pollution with the gas guzzlers we drove. Once we saw and understood it, we cooperated to change our actions. We agreed to the creation of laws to enforce our cooperation.

It makes little sense to enact laws and rules against organizational defensive routines, fancy footwork, and malaise. The equivalents of such laws are already in place, and they do not work. The answer, as in the case of prohibition, lies in each one of us becoming self-managing and helping to create organizations that reward such self-responsible actions.

Reference

Andrews, Kenneth R. 1989. *Ethics or Practice.* Boston: Harvard Business School Press.

Index

F

G

H

I

J

K

L

M

N

O

P

U

V

W

Y